what's a Christian to do ?

what's a Christian to do ?

edited by David P. Polk

Chalice Press
St. Louis, Missouri

Library of Congress Cataloging-in-Publication Data

What's a Christian to do? / edited by David Polk.
Includes bibliographical references.
1. Theology, Doctrinal—Popular works. 2. Christian ethics. 3. Process theology. I. Polk, David Patrick.
BT77.W48 1991 230'.046 91-25020
ISBN 0-8272-4229-8

Printed in the United States of America

Contents

Contributors

William A. Beardslee is professor emeritus of religion, Emory University, and director of the Process and Faith Program.

Daniel E.H. Bryant is minister of First Christian Church, Eugene, Oregon.

Judith Boice Casanova is coordinator of a dropout prevention program in La Puente, California, and the mother of a six-year-old. She was the first director of the Process and Faith Program.

John B. Cobb, Jr., is Avery Professor of Religion, Claremont Graduate School, and founding director of the Center for Process Studies

Joseph A. Deegan is an adjunct faculty member, Chapman College.

Lewis S. Ford is professor of philosophy, Old Dominion University.

David R. Griffin is professor of philosophy of religion and theology, School of Theology at Claremont and Claremont Graduate School, and a director of the Center for Process Studies.

Carol F. Johnston is an ordained minister of the Presbyterian Church in the U.S.A. and a Ph.D. candidate at Claremont Graduate School.

Jean Lambert is senior lecturer in religious studies, University of Zimbabwe.

Nelson Stringer is minister of Kailua United Methodist Church, Kailua, Hawaii.

Marjorie Suchocki is Ingraham Professor of Theology, School of Theology at Claremont, and a director of the Center for Process Studies.

Videotape Resources

Videotapes that clarify the perspective of the process theology represented in this book, and featuring several of its contributors, are available from Christian Board of Publication, P.O. Box 179, St. Louis, MO 63166. (1-800-366-3383, FAX 314-231-8524.)

What Is Process Theology? Three ten-minute segments by Marjorie Suchocki on "The Heart of Process," "Prayer and Process," and "Feminism and Process." $23.95. 34R0906.

A Relational Vision. A series of eight half-hour presentations in which John Cobb, aided by Mary Ellen Kilsby, talks about the world and faith from a process perspective. Leader's guide and 2-tape set, $75. 34R0907.

God, Power, and Process. Two segments by David Polk ("A Process View of God") and Marjorie Suchocki ("Recognizing God's Power"). 30 minutes. $23.95. 34R0908.

Human Suffering and the Power of God. Harold Kushner, author of *When Bad Things Happen to Good People*, interviewed by John Cobb. 35 minutes. $23.95. 34A0909.

How to Interpret the Bible from a Process Perspective. William Beardslee, interviewed by Nancy Howell. 35 minutes. $23.95. 34R0910.

Introduction

David P. Polk

The local school board is in turmoil. One group of parents is insisting that creationism be given equal space in science textbooks alongside the theory of evolution. A second group, just as resolute, sees no place for claims of religious faith in a public school's curriculum. What's a Christian to think?

A tragic automobile accident has claimed the lives of two popular teenagers when a drunken driver crossed the median and struck their car head-on. Parents and siblings and close friends agonize over how a loving God could have allowed so senseless a destruction of two innocent lives. What's a Christian to say?

They love each other deeply but on this issue they are painfully divided. He is marching with other protesters in front of an abortion clinic while she is at the state capitol trying to persuade her representative to oppose a bill that would outlaw almost all abortions. What's a Christian to do?

I remember fondly a whimsical poster some of my students gave me as I was ending a semester's residency with them. It portrayed an orangutan sitting forlornly against a wall, with a caption that read: "Just when I thought I knew all the answers, they changed the questions."

How often it seems to us today that this is our plight. It is not that the old answers just do not work so well any more. Rather, many of the most troubling questions hit us in new and unsettling ways. Technological, medical, and scientific advances even constantly raise new questions that challenge conventional thinking.

Amid the turmoil and confusion of competing claims of faithful response to the call of God in our lives, what *is* a Christian to do? Concerning the six topics dealt with in this book, no simple answers emerge. But there is enough food for thought here to sustain a host of hearty banquets.

The purpose that guided the writers of these chapters was not to tell each of us *what* to think and say and do but to help us in *how* we think about our beliefs and actions. Believing and understanding and doing are all interconnected in our lives. Actions arise out of convictions. Thinking helps clarify the nature of the beliefs we hold dear. *Theology* is the word that expresses this careful, reflective thinking about our faith. In that sense, then, this is a book that aims to help church folk grapple with "theological" issues in a way that will contribute to faithfulness in how we live.

Each unit is introduced by a pair of stories that vividly characterize the subject at hand. The issues at stake in the stories are then clarified, and guidance is sought from relevant biblical texts. Prevailing alternatives for dealing with the question are carefully represented, concluding with a proposed resolution that arises out of a "process" or "relational" vision of reality. Questions for reflection or discussion, and suggestions for further reading, are offered at the end of each chapter.

The eleven individuals who shared in writing these six units are all members of the Process and Faith Program of the Center for Process Studies in Claremont, California. The perspective they bring to bear on these hard issues for our times is known as "process theology," a way of understanding Christian faith that draws on the insights of the philosopher Alfred North Whitehead.

Whitehead's view of reality understands God as the ongoing power of creativity who leads the world into ever new moments of becoming. Many have found rich value in his writings because the God he depicts is in much closer harmony with biblical portrayals than the classical theism that we have inherited from past theologians. In particular, such a God is in intimate interrelation with all of creation, leading the creative advance without canceling out creaturely freedom, and feeling the pain of our mistakes with a divine passion that can genuinely be termed holy love. This God is not aloof or self-contained or "over"-powering. This God is "perfect in love," to capsulize 1 John 4:16-19.

That vision underlies the concluding sections of each of the six chapters where fresh perspective is sought for discerning how to deal with those various issues. These discussions do not depend on a prior acquaintance with this way of thinking; they intend to be self-explanatory. But persons wishing to expand their awareness of the process point of view will find especially helpful Robert Brizee's *Where in the World Is God?* (Upper Room, 1987), William Kaufman's *The Case for God* (Chalice Press, 1991), and Marjorie Suchocki's *God-Christ-Church: A Practical Guide to Process Theology* (Crossroad, rev. ed. 1989).

For persons who do not expect to find simple answers to complex issues, this book is intended. To thinking Christians who do not want someone else to tell them what to believe, this book is offered. The format lends itself well to group study. Individuals in a group or class might even "role-play" the different perspectives that surface in each chapter, or assist one another by reporting on some of the suggested reading, or enter into a more thorough Bible study of the passages discussed. The options are numerous. What is crucial, however this book is utilized, is to approach the topics and their treatment with an open mind and in an irenic spirit.

The invitation is to a journey, of discovery—possibly of faith's renewal. The objective of the journey is personal and communal enrichment, and the prospect of fresh insight into the nature of a Christian's faithful response to the unceasing call of God. May your journeying open you to new horizons of possibility.

What Can We Believe About the Bible?

Judith Boice Casanova
John B. Cobb, Jr.
Lewis S. Ford
William A. Beardslee
Joseph A. Deegan

Two Reactions to the Bible

It All Has to Be True

Phil was the first person to speak in the Christian Counseling Support Group that evening. "I have always had trouble with religion," he said. "At one time I made fun of it. But when I came to college, and I found out how little the college professors have to teach about what is right and what the meaning of life is, I began to take the Bible seriously.

"God comes alive to me alone in my room through the words of the Bible. I don't have to struggle with the question of who is right; I rest my confidence in the Bible. This gives me a firm place to stand when so many are floundering.

"It seems to me that people are flaunting the Bible, but it is my anchor in life. Science used to trouble me with its materialism and its theories of evolution. But I'm not afraid of the ways in which science seems to contradict the Bible. Science isn't the last word anyway; its point of view is constantly changing, while the Bible remains a constant.

"I try to draw sharp lines between what the Bible teaches and what the world has to offer. The Bible opens the way to a new and fuller life, and one that I am eager to share with others.

"Finally, several of you invited me to these group counseling sessions. I'm not sure how far I can go in counseling with you, because so many of you do not share my point of view. But I've decided to try one meeting with you, to see whether I can believe that God is working with you or not."

One Book Among Many?

"I find it interesting, Phil, that you speak as you do of the Bible," said Marilyn, whose turn to talk came later in the evening. "This is my first experience in a Christian therapy group. I came here to find some direction again. When I was a child, my parents instilled into me the Bible's authority. But somehow in the free thinking of my college years, I ignored it as a guide for my life. The Bible, I thought, is only one book among many that represent the sum total of human wisdom. And it is an ancient book at that. Surely there were available to me more up-to-date, relevant insights.

"I was confident that my own reason could distinguish truth from error, whether in the Bible or anywhere else. When I experienced trouble in my life, I studied literature, philosophy, and psychology for insights to help me. Then for a time, different religious movements and self-help books provided me with answers. But I found these answers always temporary. And when they conflicted, I had a hard time deciding which one was right. I began to realize I sought a single, guiding truth in my life.

"But my Bible isn't like Phil's. I've begun to study the Bible seriously again. But I don't expect it to be sure all the way, and I don't expect it to agree with modern science.

Jesus—his words and what he did—this is the core of the Bible for me. There I find a truth that is absolute for me. I am working on how to relate that truth to the world we are learning about in college, and I have a long way to go. But I too have a foundation, though it is a very different one from Phil's."

The Authority of the Bible

Changing Attitudes

All Christians understand the central role played by the Bible in the life of faith. On the questions of the extent of the Bible's authority, however, they differ greatly. For some, the Bible is the exclusive source of that truth that ultimately matters in life. In the first of the foregoing stories, Phil has found what seems to him a clear authority, spelled out in a great deal of detail.

In a very different way, Marilyn has been finding an authority in the Bible. She has come to believe that much of it is no longer authoritative, but she finds in the Jesus of the Gospels a figure where God's examples are the permanently valid, authoritative part of the Bible.

The Bible and Lifestyles

The stories of Phil and Marilyn show clearly that the question of biblical authority is much more than a dry, intellectual one. The attitudes they had adopted toward it were both a result and a cause of their total lifestyles. Psychological, emotional, and spiritual factors had been involved in their personal difficulties. Phil and Marilyn began from different angles to work through the Bible's authority in their lives. For Phil this meant accepting biblical authoritarianism. For Marilyn it meant finding a core of truth in the Bible.

How Does God Communicate?

Behind the question of the Bible's authority stand differing views of God's active communication to human beings. Does God speak to us directly in the events of our present lives, or only through the medium of a book written centuries ago? And what does it mean that the Bible is the inspired Word of God? Everyone recognizes that human writers produced the various books of the Bible. To call the Bible inspired, then, might mean that the work of these writers was greatly influenced by God, though still prone to errors of fact and judgment, as all human work is.

Or the inspiration of the Bible might mean that, in a symbolic sense, God actually "wrote" it—that is, that God so overwhelmed its human writers as to make them perfect instruments of divine communication. Agreement with this second alternative usually underlies belief in the Bible's infallibility. For the Bible to be infallible, it would have to be a perfectly direct revelation of a Being who cannot err.

The words *liberal* and *literal* have become labels in the church for the two ways of interpreting the Bible and its authority that we are indicating here. Let us now listen to how each argues its own case and readily finds weaknesses in the opposing viewpoint.

The Literal View

The Inspired Word of God

The Bible is the inspired Word of God. As such, it is our anchor and compass for life in the twentieth century as much as in any other age. Without a sure knowledge of and a firm belief in the tenets of the Bible, we drift like unclaimed wreckage, tossed to and fro by every current and wave of the secular sea around us. Unfortunately, however, this truth has been lost to many people who see in the Bible nothing but an interesting historical record.

A high view of the Bible's inspiration does not determine a single theory about it. One possibility is "verbal inspiration," which means that God's Spirit guided the writers of the Bible so closely that there were no errors of any kind in the original writings. Another is "plenary inspiration," which means that the Bible reveals everything necessary to our salvation. It is not intended to be an authority about everything. We need not turn to it for scientific data or for accuracy of historical details. But we do need to turn to it for the authoritative revelation of God and God's will, because we need the definite guidance of the word of God, since we cannot know God in any clear way without it.

The Safeguard of Faith

These high views of the Bible's inspiration and authority have kept the Bible close to the center of vision of the world of believers, so that it could help to shape that vision. They have given confidence and strength to Christians faced by doubt and despair. They have brought the message of justice and love from an ancient book into the modern world. Think what would have happened to the Christian faith if close adherence to the Bible had not guided its journey through the ages to the present time. Perhaps as early as the third or fourth century, all accurate recollection of Jesus' life and of his teaching would have been lost. Instead, weak memories and skewed interpretations would have so distorted the meaning of Christ that its connection with the Jesus who really lived would no longer have existed.

Our Need for the Bible

If we humans could achieve our salvation through our own reason and will, then surely the Son of God never would have come into the world to die. But not only are we too weak-willed to save ourselves, we cannot even recognize what's good for us. There is a baffling confusion of opinion among poets, psychologists, philosophers, and scientists about what brings happiness or offers the most fulfilling ways of life. One becomes even more confused by considering the paths advocated by the many religions of the world. Beyond this is the problem of the world itself, which is in such a moral darkness that any hope of recognizing God in it has been lost.

It is Jesus who is the Way, the Truth, and the Life. We know this not just by the arguments of reason, but as a fundamental conviction of faith. It is a truth reported in the Bible, which may be considered God's own self-revelation. That is something indispensable for us, since our finite minds alone cannot grasp the Infinite Being of God. We are totally dependent upon the Bible for our knowledge of God and God's purposes in the world.

The Bible's Infallible Truth

Despite its human writers, we can assume that the Bible contains no significant error. If we are going to believe in the Bible as God's Word, we must be able to trust the accuracy of this Word. Of course, we are not talking about minor inconsistencies or trivial detail that might, with no consequence, be errors of the human writers. Some examples of this kind can be found in both the Old and New Testaments. It is different, however, in regard to essential matters of faith. These have to do with the self-revelation of God and the Creator to whom we owe everything, with God's will for the way we live, with God's revelation in Jesus Christ, and with God's promises regarding our ultimate destiny. Concerning these matters at the very least, we can be certain that the Bible is God's infallible Word. For we must know the truth about them if we are to have eternal life in Christ. And it is inconceivable that God would allow the Bible to deceive us concerning our salvation.

Well grounded in our assurance of the truth of biblical teaching, we are prepared to proclaim God's Word confidently to others. How many there are who have not yet believed that Jesus Christ died for our sins, that trusting in him, we find forgiveness and new life! As believers in God's Word found reliably in the whole of scripture, we are emboldened and empowered to carry out the great commission to preach the gospel to every creature.

The Liberal View

The Effects of Biblical Scholarship

Throughout most of Christian history, the Bible was taken as generally trustworthy. Until the 1830s no one had effectively challenged that consensus. But at that point, geological investigations questioned the shortness of the past assumed by Bible readers, and later Darwin's evolutionary theory threw doubt on many details of the Genesis creation stories. Meanwhile, rigorous biblical scholars noticed all sorts of anomalies and discrepancies that could best be explained by multiple authorship of individual books. In particular, these studies questioned whether Moses wrote the first five books of the Hebrew Scriptures, and they also questioned whether original disciples of Jesus wrote the Gospels.

Today, biblical scholars examine the Bible in much the same way that they study other works of ancient literature. For they fully recognize that the Bible too had human writers whose perspectives were limited and shaped by the historical times in which they lived. No one should be surprised any longer to learn of contradictions and mistakes within the Bible. Nor should anyone doubt that the Bible is filled with ancient ways of thinking that we no longer share today.

What Lies Behind the Claim of Inerrancy?

The case for biblical inerrancy is not usually based on the rearguard action of refuting the seeming discrepancies in the scriptures. The claim of inerrancy is based primarily on an assumption about divine power: The best sort of power a perfect being can exercise is unilateral, controlling power. God is able to accomplish God's purposes single-handedly. If God has this kind of power, God will see to it that the Bible expresses an unambiguous message to humanity.

By the same logic, it is easy to see, God should be able to prevent most of the evil and suffering in the world. For most of those who suffer, this is a far more acute problem. Many argue that God can, and even will, do away with all such evil and suffering, but God allows them to continue for the present in order to permit the exercise of human freedom. Against this, one may suggest: If evil and suffering are tolerated for the sake of human freedom, shouldn't this same freedom to make mistakes show up in the formation and transmission of scripture?

The Heart of the Bible

Though we cannot accept the Bible as an authority that is valid throughout, the heart of the Bible speaks strongly to us. We listen to the message of Jesus about God's love, and read about what he did to express God's love, and we find in this central part of the Bible the focus of our faith. It is very important to distinguish this core from the outdated world view and morality and theology that color so much of scripture. Only in this way can we present a convincing message that truly leads the hearer to God.

Interpretation and Freedom

Thus, in contrast to the literal interpretation, we need not assume that God completely overwhelmed the humanity of the biblical authors in their efforts to put God's Word into writing. If we live with life's suffering, so also do we live with ambiguity in the scriptures. Both derive from the freedom to be human.

In several other important respects, the literal interpretation of the Bible is an attack on freedom, divine as well as human. It prescribes the one and only way of God's communication to human beings. God's freedom to speak to us outside or in contradiction to the Bible is denied. And the human attempt to find God's truth in the world when the Bible seems archaic is pronounced invalid. In regard to behavior, the Bible is turned into a legalistic rule book that supplants autonomous decision. In regard to knowledge, it is used to censor scientific and historical investigation. The literal interpretation heightens the Bible's authority to an absurd extreme.

The Bible as a Book of Liberation

The most important way of hearing the Bible today is to let it speak as a record of the struggle of God and human beings for liberation. This is important because it is what poor, oppressed people are finding in it.

Most readers of this discussion will not be from among the poor and oppressed. We may not be affluent, but we live in a wealthy country, and our situation gifts us with a standard of living that is high among all the people of the earth. Without thinking much about it, we are among the heaviest consumers anywhere of both raw materials and manufactured goods. What does it mean to us to read the Bible as a book of liberation?

A first answer from many parts of the Bible, both from the Hebrew Scriptures and from the New Testament, is that being as privileged as we are, economically, is a very dangerous position. The Hebrew laws, the prophets, the wisdom books, and especially the words of Jesus in the Gospels warn us that our apparent security makes it very likely that we shall miss the point of life.

Next, the Bible leads us to realize that we are deeply at one with the oppressed, the poor, and the suffering. We may forget this, but it is the reality of our life. If we read the Bible seriously, we will learn to listen to the voices of these who seem to us to be outsiders, those whose place is very different from our own.

Then, if we see ourselves in the story of liberation, which the Bible tells, we shall have to ask ourselves how we can live differently, so as to take part in the story of the liberation of life to which the Bible orients us.

An Old Testament Perspective on the Bible as the Word of God

> Now they told...David, "The Philistines are fighting against Keilah, and are robbing the threshing floors." David inquired of the LORD, "Shall I go and attack these Philistines?" The LORD said to David, "Go and attack the Philistines and save Keilah"....So David and his men went to Keilah, fought with the Philistines,...and dealt them a heavy defeat. Thus David rescued the inhabitants of Keilah....
>
> David said, "O LORD, the God of Israel, your servant has heard that Saul seeks to come to Keilah, to destroy the city on my account. And now, will Saul come down as your servant has heard? O LORD, the God of Israel, I beseech you, tell your servant." The LORD said, "He will come down." Then David said,

> "Will the men of Keilah surrender me and my men into the hand of Saul?" The LORD said, "They will surrender you." Then David and his men, who were about six hundred, set out and left Keilah....When Saul was told that David had escaped from Keilah, he gave up the expedition.
>
> 1 Samuel 23:1–13

David at Keilah

Hearing and acting on God's word has always been a priority for the men and women of God. However, what one hears and how one acts on that word has never been quite as agreed upon as the original need to hear and do. For many, hearing and acting on God's word has come to mean how one responds to the words and spirit of the Bible. Perhaps, then, an incident from the Bible can help us as we seek to hear and act on God's word as found in that Bible.

This incident tells of one event in the life of David, who had been anointed by Samuel as the future king of Israel, but who, at this moment, was an outlaw with a price on his head. He has fled into the desert to save his own skin and has been joined by about six hundred other outlaws and convicted criminals. Think of Robin Hood without the benefits of Sherwood Forest and Maid Marian. Outlaw or not, David considers himself God's person and is actively trying to seek and do God's will. At God's urging, David leaves his relatively safe desert "hole" and, with his men, liberates the besieged city of Keilah. King Saul, David's arch enemy, is overjoyed that David has left his "hiding hole" and proposes to shut him up in the walled city of Keilah. Before he can do so, however, David hears of the scheme.

Now, there were a lot of possibilities open to David. He could have assumed that because God had sent him to Keilah, God would certainly take care of him there. He also could have assumed that since he, not Saul, had delivered Keilah from the Philistines, the people of Keilah would protect and defend him. He even could have assumed that, as God's anointed, he could—with God's help, of course—triumph over Saul as he had over the Philistines.

What he did was go right back to God, and once again he heard God's word: Saul is coming, and the men of Keilah will deliver you up to him. And David, man of God that he was, rather than working with God's word to ensure that it happened, worked with God's word to ensure that it *didn't* happen. He scrambled out of town as fast as he could, and Saul never bothered to pay Keilah that royal visit.

Reflections on the Story

First, walking with God is a moment-by-moment consultation. It is an ongoing relationship, not a dependency on past word or words. While the Bible is certainly profitable for study, reproof, correction, and for training in righteousness (2 Timothy 3:16), the person who plants himself or herself firmly on a text is urging others toward a proposed position or course of action that is on shaky ground.

Second, God's word is not a "sentence," the word spoken that *must be* fulfilled regardless of consequences or interim action. God said to David, Saul will come up and the men of Keilah will surrender you. But in point of fact, Saul did not come up, and the men of Keilah did not surrender David.

Third, as we look at our world in the light of the biblical prophecies that point to Armageddon and the destruction of the world by fire, the link with the arms race and nuclear proliferation may seem obvious. But if the story of David at Keilah has any relevance for us, it is surely to point out that prophecy need not be fulfilled. For as we act in a creative response to the Word, we may negate that very word and the word of death may become, by our response, the word of life. (The parallel with Jonah and Nineveh is further evidence of this possibility.) Oh, that we may hear God's word and, when appropriate, scramble to avoid it half as fast as David did!

A Process Perspective on the Bible

Someone impressed by the concepts of Alfred North Whitehead who adopts a "process" way of thinking does not find the question of how one will view the authority of the

Bible to be a settled matter. But helpful guidelines for Christians who think about this question do emerge.

The Role of the Past

First, process thinkers see that the present includes the past. What we are now is largely shaped by what we and our ancestors have been. But we do not think of these primarily as our biological ancestors. When Lincoln said that our forefathers had brought forth this nation, his words were valid for those whose biological ancestors had not yet come to this country fourscore and seven years earlier. Similarly, those of us who are white North American Christians see our spiritual ancestry as lying with Israel, even though most of our biological ancestors were in the forests of northern Europe at the time. The whole past influences us, but within the past there are some to whom we are chiefly indebted. We identify ourselves by a certain story of what *we* have done and what has happened to *us*. For Christians, the most important part of that story is told in the Bible.

Discerning the Leading of God

Second, process thinkers think that God is a part of everything that happens. Everyone lives, in fact, by the grace and providence of God. But some block the effectiveness of God's work in their lives by denying or ignoring it. Grace and guidance become much more effective when we believe in God and trust God. Similarly, there is an element of inspiration in all real thinking. Without the Holy Spirit, we would have no insight into truth at all! But that inspiration becomes much more effective when people acknowledge it and attune themselves to it. Of all ancient writers, it was especially those of Israel who listened for God's word and sought to share it with others. Jews and Christians have not been wrong to claim a special inspiration for their writings.

The Influences of the Creatures

Third, process thinkers believe that worldly influence and human decision also play a part in everything that happens. No event is *simply* God's doing. In every event, creatures, too, have played a role, sometimes remarkably responsive to God's call and leading, sometimes pathetically rebellious. In every event, the actual historical situation plays a very large role as well. Hence, no event, including the writing of the sentences of which our scriptures are composed, can be seen as expressive only of God's inspiration. The historical situation and human decision also play a role.

The Fallibility of Human Efforts

Fourth, only God is omniscient, and only God is infallible. Every creaturely event and product is finite and fallible. The human effort to claim inerrancy for some human being or some created object, whether Bible or pope or church creed, expresses a refusal to let God be God and fails to acknowledge the limitations of creaturehood.

Interest More Important Than Accuracy

Fifth, the primary question about ideas or propositions is not whether they are accurate. More important is whether these ideas or propositions capture human attention, provide new ways of understanding the world, and open us to new insights. When we strive simply for accuracy, we are likely to come out with dull and unimportant statements. Stories and poems are often more life-giving than a strictly accurate recital of facts. On the other hand, truth adds to interest. We want stories and poems that relate significantly to reality at some level. The story need not be an exact statement of what really happened, but for it to move us and expand our horizons, it needs to be believable and to draw us into it. We may learn more about the past through a historical novel than through a textbook in history. But that will occur only if the author has captured the mood or spirit of the time with some accuracy.

Biblical Authority

These points give us a basis for thinking about biblical authority. First, we will not approach the Bible in the same way that we approach any other ancient document. This is for the same reason that I do not approach my own past life with the same attitude that I approach the life of another.

I am related to my own personal past inwardly. And we Christians are related to our collective past inwardly. We may use some of the same techniques in studying our own past as in studying the past of others, but the whole approach is not the same.

When we think of it this way, we see that it will not do to extract a kernel or core of authoritative truth from the Bible. The whole biblical witness is important for us. The sins, failures, and confusions of which it speaks are part of who we are as a community still struggling to be faithful!

The alternative to viewing biblical authority as being the same as that of any other ancient writings is not to understand the Bible as infallible. Nothing is infallible except God. We may speak very strongly of our conviction that the biblical writings are inspired—inspired, perhaps, as nothing else has ever been—but we cannot move from inspiration to infallibility. To treat anything creaturely as infallible is to move dangerously close to *idolatry*, the worship of something that is creaturely.

What is important is that we not take the question of literal accuracy as the focus of our attention. The major function of divine inspiration of human thought and writing is not to preserve it from factual errors. On the contrary, inspiration is much more related to insight and imagination than to exact recording of objective facts. It is the insights and images, brought into fruitful contrast with the ideas and meaning of the modern world, that have the power to liberate, heal, and empower us today. But these insights and images would not liberate, heal, and empower if they were not profoundly true. We can never set aside the question of truth.

The familiar arguments about the authority of the Bible have been about whether the definite facts and clear ideas of the Bible were correct. Perhaps it is a good time to put this sort of question on the back burner, so to speak, and ask a different sort of question. The discussion will point us to important issues that we tend to miss if we accept the traditional way of talking about the Bible's authority.

Suppose we think of the Bible as proposing to us a different kind of world from the one in which we live. Then we will be asking, "How would our world be changed if we let it be touched by the world of the Bible? How would we be changed?"

These are not new questions, but they have far too often been obscured by the debates about historical accuracy and verbal inspiration in the discussion of what the Bible means. Also, these are questions that will make a difference in what we hear or learn from the Bible. And when we ask the question about how our world would be changed if we let it be touched by the world of the Bible, we will find that we would not want to be guided by everything that is in the Bible. We shall be in a conversation with it, in which we listen very seriously to what it proposes.

The Bible and God in Process Thought

As we noted earlier, one of the main issues with which Christians have struggled as they tried to understand the Bible was the question of divine power. Process thinkers have questioned whether any cosmic, all-inclusive power ought to be or could be "unilateral," working only from one side. Unilateral power cancels out the effectiveness of other powers. Finite unilateral powers can co-exist, each having a bit of the action, but an infinite unilateral action would preclude all others. For that reason, this understanding of power has been used quite sparingly in traditional theology: in the initial creation, when no other beings are supposed to be, and in the final consummation, where the existence of finite powers could seem to be problematic. A better way of thinking would be to reconceive divine cosmic power as a power that works *with* the powers of the world to achieve its ends indirectly. Such power is persuasive rather than controlling.

What we see in evolution points to one such power in the world: our past heritage. There is ample basis for supposing that the more complex organisms have emerged out of simpler ones. On the other hand, evolutionary power is often suspect, to religious people, because of the place of chance in it, that is, random mutation. Could not God's creative role be reconciled with this evidence of a history of development by conceiving it to be a persuasive, directive agency that seeks the emergence of more complex organisms, while at the same time respecting and using the powers of that which is already existent?

Of course, the evidence for the gradual emergence of the complex from the simple is an embarrassment for those who think that God created materially by the direct exercise of God's will. On the other hand, if God creates by persuasion, using the powers that already exist, we should expect an evolutionary development. In the same way, if God caused the Bible to come into being over a millennium through the dedicated efforts of many individuals, this work of God, this divine causation, is best understood as persuasive and contributory, not as ultimately controlling. We should expect some errors to creep in, as part of the human contribution to the process, remembering the adage, "To err is human." We ought to be surprised if it were otherwise.

Christians as People of the Book

Christians are people of the book. It cannot be otherwise. If we turn away from the Bible, we cease to be who we are. But one thing that is particularly remarkable about this book is that again and again it exposes human pretenses, especially the pretenses of those who claim a special relation to God. It does not absolutize itself, and it certainly does not conceal the sins and stupidities of Jews and Christians. To be people of the book is to be a people who know that the history that makes us who we are is one of both greatness and shame, of both devotion and betrayal. As heirs of that history, we find both greatness and shame within ourselves as well, both devotion and betrayal. The revelatory power of the Bible includes its exposure of our pretenses. It enables us to acknowledge our sin and yet live in the joy of grace. The authority of the Bible lies in its continuing power to give us an identity that frees us to acknowledge the truth about ourselves and our world, and about the Bible as well. That authority is betrayed when we try to safeguard it by attributing to the ancient writers an infallibility they never claimed.

Questions for Discussion

1. Where as Christians do we look for authority? How do we relate that authority to our own responsibility?

2. Do we expect that we shall always hear the same things from the Bible?

3. If you were to criticize your own way of reading the Bible, what would you say?

4. What are the one or two most important things that the Bible means to you?

5. What do you think that the work of biblical scholars contributes to your reading and understanding of the Bible?

6. What do you find the Bible saying about God's power?

7. Is the Bible more interested in what people believe, or in what they do?

8. What does the Bible contribute to your understanding of who you are?

9. Whether you are reading the Bible, or pondering God's will for the critical issues of your own life and of our common life together, do you expect to hear from God a definite prediction of how things are going to come out?

For Further Reading

Achtemeier, Paul, *The Inspiration of Scripture.* Westminster Press, 1980. Like this chapter, Achtemeier finds weaknesses in both liberal and conservative views.

Blaisdell, Charles, ed., *Conservative—Moderate—Liberal: The Biblical Authority Debate.* CBP Press, 1991. A remarkable engagement between representatives of widely differing views of biblical authority.

Ford, Lewis S., *The Lure of God.* Fortress Press, 1978. Ford finds in the Bible strong support for the process view of God as lurer and persuader.

Kelsey, David H., *The Uses of Scripture in Recent Theology.* Fortress Press, 1975. A full but rather technical description of how recent theologians have used the Bible.

Marshall, I. Howard, *I Believe in the Historical Jesus.* William B. Eerdmans Publishing Company, 1977. A thoughtful, conservative work. Though it focuses on Jesus rather than on the Bible as a whole, it raises fundamental questions about biblical inspiration from the point of view of a conservative evangelical.

How Are God and Evolution Related?

David R. Griffin
Joseph A. Deegan

Competing Views of Evolution: Two Stories

It Makes Me Feel Like a Robot

Jim knew Dr. Helen Jordan at church as a woman of strong faith and commitment to the Christian community. He had only recently learned that she also was a well-known scientist who had done ground-breaking research in human brain physiology. Out of curiosity about her work, he decided to attend a lecture she was giving at the state university on the latest developments in her field.

Much of the lecture was over Jim's head. But it fascinated him nonetheless and troubled him a lot. For it seemed to Jim that all her science was framed in the theory of evolution. How often she began her statements with words such as "In the evolution of the brain...," or "As the brain evolved...."

In the question-and-answer session following the lecture, several people spoke critically of belief in evolution. Jim, too, raised his hand to speak. "If my brain," he said, "is only a system of chemical adaptations to the environment, it makes me feel like nothing but a robot. I deeply believe I'm more significant than that."

When the evening was over, Jim and Helen greeted each other as friends. But Jim was angry. "How can you leave your Christian faith at home, or in church," Jim asked, "when you come here to speak of something so valuable as our human brain? Or don't you *really* believe that God is our Creator?"

"I don't think you understand the way science works, Jim," said Helen. "When I do science, I have to follow its rules for finding truth. Our Christian faith is another world of truth—a higher truth, I agree, but still a different kind of truth."

But Jim's mind was firm. "The Bible has explained God's creation. In the book of Genesis, God created the world and God created us, and God created us directly. And there can be only one truth," he replied heatedly.

Conflict over School Books

The battle over science textbooks had subsided in the school district after a new set of texts had been chosen several years earlier. All parties had agreed to accept texts that attempted to sidestep controversy by avoiding the theory of evolution.

Now the battle was to heat up again as school board members Juanita Fuller and Robert Abernathy prepared a challenge to the so-called "compromise" textbooks.

The two board members met one day to prepare their arguments. They agreed that the publishers of the new textbooks had too easily surrendered to the demands of creationists when they eliminated all references to evolution from their presentations of current scientific knowledge. Now the textbooks were so watered down that high school students could not learn many of the essential facts about modern science from them.

"I'm glad we agree on this," said Ms. Fuller to her colleague, "but it does bother me that you see evolution as removing God entirely from our understanding of the universe. Wouldn't the best explanation be one that sees God using evolution in the creation of the world?"

"But science itself doesn't support belief in God," said Mr. Abernathy. "Science looks for empirical facts. It has yet to find the fact, or collection of facts, called God. I have to conclude, therefore, that God does not exist. Plenty of facts support evolution, but none support God. The science textbooks we choose should communicate to students only the conclusions that scientific fact supports."

Evolution Today: A Spectrum of Views

The Legacy of Darwin

Ever since Charles Darwin published *The Origin of Species* in 1859, the battle lines between modern science and a literal interpretation of the Bible have been drawn. *Creationism* is a common name for the view that the six-day creation of the world by God related in the book of Genesis is the one and only true account of the world's origins. Following Darwin, in contrast, modern science understands that the present state of the world arose through an evolutionary process taking billions of years.

Two Different Authorities

If students today are to learn science, they surely must be taught to understand how crucial a role the theory of evolution plays in the work of modern scientists. This is the conviction shared by school board members Robert Abernathy and Juanita Fuller in the vignette, "Conflict over School Books." Abernathy goes on to reveal that his own affirmation of the theory of evolution involves a corresponding denial that God exists. He is an atheist. The reasoning by which he denies God's existence is based on the authority of scientific method, which requires all knowledge to derive from observable facts. Stated crudely, science observes God nowhere, so Abernathy won't believe God exists.

For Jim, however, in "It Makes Me Feel Like a Robot," the ultimate authority in all things is the Bible. He cannot possibly accept the modern theory of evolution because it contradicts the Genesis account of creation. He is a creationist. He does not understand how his sister in faith, Helen Jordan, can profess God the Creator in church on Sunday and the theory of evolution during her workday week.

Evolution and Meaning

In Jim's highly charged reaction to Helen's lecture, the question of life's meaning also arises. Jim feels deeply that to understand himself in any way as a product of evolution would rob him of the sense of his life's value. His faith gives him the assurance of being a child of God, of being vastly more significant than a mechanical product of nature.

In confessing to the Christian faith as a "higher truth," Helen acknowledges that she shares a similar vision of her own worth. But she seems to have insulated this positive experience of life's meaning from the mechanistic aspects of her scientific conclusions about the human brain. In science, Helen finds objective truth about humans as participants in nature, while in Christian faith she finds meaning and value. Although she affirms both evolution and God, she sees no relation between them.

Creation as Evolution

Of the four characters in the two stories, Juanita Fuller is the only one to relate evolution and God in a positive way. But she only hints to her school board colleague at a possible understanding of God's creation as evolution. The final section of this chapter consists of a fuller elaboration of such a view. It spells out a way of thinking by which one might positively respond to the question, "How are God and evolution related?" Preceding it are three negative answers to the same question, i.e., the answers of creationism, atheism, and Christian existentialism.

The question that these positions answer is a uniquely modern one. Yet, the perspective of the Bible on the creation of the world is clearly relevant to its discussion. Thus, before considering whether God and evolution are related at all, let us hear in the following section about the Bible's own view of creation.

Creation in the Bible

Dependence on God

On the most fundamental level, the Bible's statements about creation assert that nothing in this world stands on its own power, that all that exists is dependent upon God for its being. No only did God create the world "in the beginning," but God continues to preserve it in every moment. If God should withhold the divine breath from any of us, we would immediately be reduced to dust (Job 34:1; Psalm 104:29).

The most famous and extensive biblical passage dealing with creation is the first two chapters of the book of Genesis. But there are abundant references to creation scattered throughout the Bible. Besides Genesis 1 and 2, three other groups of material are important. They are the Wisdom literature, especially Proverbs, Job, and a number of "wisdom" psalms; the hymnic praises and thanksgiving for God's "handiwork" in the Psalms; and the writings of the prophet known as Second Isaiah, who lived during Israel's Babylonian exile, and whose work is found in the book of Isaiah beginning at chapter 40. We will end with a discussion of the Genesis account after briefly reviewing this other material.

Seeing God's Glory in Creation

The Bible's primary subject matter is God's redemption of the human community through history. Wisdom literature stands out in the scriptures by its relative lack of interest in this topic. It is more concerned to witness to the glory of God that can be seen directly in the works of creation. The Wisdom writers have thoughtfully contemplated nature, looking for its secret, and they have been moved to profound admiration.

> The LORD by wisdom founded the earth;
>   by understanding he established the heavens;
> by his knowledge the deeps broke open,
>   and the clouds drop down the dew.
>
> Proverbs 3:19–20

The wisdom and understanding of God reflected visibly in the creation command the most profound awe. Such thoughtful contemplation of "the works of thy fingers" can provoke wonder and raise the question why, in this great creation, God is mindful of human beings at all, though the psalmist goes on to celebrate the dignity of the human creation (Psalm 8).

God Both Creates and Cares

A number of psalms do make a connection between God's care for the human community and God's work in nature. Psalm 136 asks us to thank the God who has done the great wonders of nature *and* has brought Israel out of Egypt and into the promised land. These very different acts are comparable and even continuous in that both belong to the divine creative work as a whole.

The Struggle Against Chaos

In the Psalms and elsewhere in the Bible, a common way to conceive God's creative work is through the picture of a victorious struggle against chaos, occasionally personified in the names Rahab or Leviathan (see Psalm 89:9–10). In thinking like this, the Bible expresses an understanding of creation as a perpetually unfolding rescue of the world from forces of negativity and formlessness. Whether in history or nature, God's creative acts also are saving acts, "manifestations of Yahweh's favor" (Psalm 89:1). In Psalm 74, creation becomes salvation:

> Yet God my king is from of old,
>   working salvation in the earth.
> You divided the sea by your might;
>   you broke the heads of the dragons in the waters.
> You crushed the heads of Leviathan....
> You cut openings for springs and torrents;....

Yours is the day, yours also the night;
you established the luminaries and the sun.
You have fixed all the bounds of the earth;
you made summer and winter.
Psalm 74:12-17

One Redemptive Purpose

It is Second Isaiah who most forcefully insists on the continuity between the creation and salvation through history that together shall fulfill one redemptive purpose. In looking forward to a new act of God in the prophet's own time, the return of Israel to Jerusalem, he says:

Awake, awake, put on strength,
O arm of the LORD!
Awake, as in days of old....
Was it not you who cut Rahab in pieces,
who pierced the dragon?
Was it not you who dried up the sea,
the waters of the great deep;
Who made the depths of the sea a way
for the redeemed to cross over?
Isaiah 51:9-10

Second Isaiah repeatedly alludes to God's creation and saving works in the past to encourage his hearers to trust God to liberate them from the most recent forces of chaos. For this prophet, God's redemption of the human community began in creation and continues through Israel's history.

The Genesis Accounts

The presentation of creation in Genesis 1 and 2 is based on a similar point of view. Although it gives the strong first impression that creation was finished by the "seventh day," it actually includes the opening series of events in a much longer story. The point of speaking of the six days of God's work was to show that creation took place within time, not before it. As such, these six days are continuous with the history of the human community down to the life of Israel in the promised land. The creation of the physical universe is the first act, but far from the last, in God's liberation of the world from the forces of chaos. Even the first verses of Genesis witness to this liberation from chaos. Under the traditional translation—"In the beginning, God created the heavens and the earth"—these verses have been used to support the idea of creation out of nothing, instead of out of chaos. But a more accurate rendering of the Hebrew is, "When God began creating the heavens and the earth, the earth was without form and void...."

There are clearly two stories of creation in the opening chapters of Genesis. The first extends from Genesis 1:1 to 2:4a, the second from 2:4b to 2:25. In both of these stories, the original creation reaches its culmination in the appearance of the first man and woman. The very purpose of creation is seen as bringing forth these beings "made in the image and likeness of God" (Genesis 1:26–27; 5:1). The work is perfect until the human pair sins, bringing the return of chaos in the form of the consequences of sin. But God does not leave the world to the dragons of chaos. There is hope for the world, for God has created and continues to create it in every era.

Of course, the biblical writers were not thinking of evolution! But they were far more aware of the intimate connection between the human world and the whole of creation, and of the continuing engagement of God in re-creating the world, than much of our Bible interpretation has shown.

We turn now to four contemporary viewpoints on God and evolution, culminating with the presentation of a positive relationship of the two from a process perspective.

How Are God and Evolution Related?

I. Not at All: A Creationist's Answer

Opposing Worldviews

The idea of God and the idea of evolution cannot be related. They belong to two completely different worldviews and philosophies of life. The Bible clearly states that God created the world out of nothing (*ex nihilo*). The theory of evolution denies this. It believes that the world has always existed. It says that nature evolved into its present state, with its complex forms of life, out of a very simple, chaotic state of pre-existent materials. Evolutionism claims that nature did this on its own, without any supernatural guidance. It is a naturalistic, atheistic philosophy, having no room for divine creation or even divine providence. To believe in evolution is to be an atheist.

Since creationism is the doctrine taught by the Bible, some people claim that it is a "religious" view, whereas evolutionism is the "scientific" view. But that is false. Both views are religious, and both are scientific.

Both Views Are Religious

Why are both views religious? Because neither one can be proven; either one or the other must be taken on faith. For example, the evolutionist must take it on faith that this beautifully and intricately complex creation has come about entirely by chance. That takes more faith than to believe that, if enough airplane parts were scattered on the beach, a windstorm could construct a Boeing 747 out of them! Of course, the evolutionist claims that the seemingly impossible is possible if there is enough time—that's one reason the evolutionist tries to prove that the earth is several billions of years old. But could a windstorm construct an airplane out of scrap parts even if it had four billion years? Another element of faith in the evolutionist's creed is the notion that all things of value, including the human mind, were inherent in the subatomic particles from which the world was created. Does it take more faith to believe in an omnipotent creator than to believe that consciousness, freedom, and love were present in electrons, protons, and neutrons? No, evolutionism is based on faith as much as creationism is.

Both Views Are Scientific

But both views are also scientific. A scientific view is one that explains all or at least most of the facts in question. Creationism can explain most of the facts, once its basic hypothesis is granted. In my view, it explains the facts better than evolutionism. I do not have time to justify this claim here, but there are many books in which these issues are thoroughly discussed.

Atoms Can Never Be Moral

There is no question more important than the choice between these two worldviews, since they lead to completely different philosophies of life. Evolutionism says that we are nothing but a very complex organization of atoms. But atoms are amoral. If evolutionism is correct, then we are amoral too. (The amoral cannot become moral merely by becoming "very complex.") Evolutionism says that the universe is ruled by blind, purposeless chance and necessity. This leads to a nihilistic philosophy of life, according to which our lives are devoid of all meaning and purpose. Evolutionism says that all progress has come about by the competitive struggle for survival based on force. If this is the highest law of the universe, it leads to the conclusion, as it did for Hitler and Mussolini, that war is the way to improve the human race. Evolutionism leads to an amoral, nihilistic, militaristic philosophy of life. Either we choose evolution and its empty, meaningless world, or we choose God.

Baptizing Evolution Doesn't Work

Of course, there are those who try to baptize evolution, speaking of "theistic evolution." But this is a self-contradictory expression. Theism is supernaturalism, while evolution is naturalism. Theistic evolutionism would therefore be "supernatural naturalism." In other words, the so-called theistic evolutionist says that our world was created out of a pre-existent chaos, while theism says that the world was created *ex nihilo*. One cannot be both a theist and an evolutionist.

Furthermore, the so-called theistic evolutionist is trying to save the biblical faith in God by making it compatible with evolution, even though the Bible itself shows that God created the world *ex nihilo,* in six days, a few thousand years ago. The theistic evolutionist denies these and many other biblical ideas, such as the facts that the first woman was created out a bone from the side of the first man, and that this first pair was created perfect and subsequently fell from grace. If all of these fundamental ideas of the Bible are rejected as false, there is no reason to believe any other parts of the biblical revelation. And in fact, theistic evolutionism is not a stable position; it is simply a resting place between theism and full-fledged atheism.

Truly, God and evolution cannot be combined. We should not try to join together what God and biblical revelation have put asunder!

II. Not at All: An Atheist's Answer

To ask how God and evolution are related presupposes that they are both real. But there are many good reasons to believe in evolution and none for believing in God. There are good reasons *not* to believe in God, and evolution is one of them.

Evidence Refutes Creationism

Unlike that fuzzy-minded hybrid called a "theist evolutionist," the creationist at least sees that theism and evolutionism are diametrically opposed. This means that the debate with the creationist can be very brief. The evidence for the fact that the world is several billion years old, not merely a few thousand, and that complex forms of life which now exist evolved out of simpler ones, is so abundant and so convincing that it is almost pointless to argue the case with one who has rejected this evidence. However, I will mention one particularly convincing type of evidence.

Creationists believe that the various species (or what they call "kinds") of plants and animals were created *ex nihilo*, in their present forms. But there is a great deal of evidence to refute this view. For example, one reason that we humans have so many back problems is that our spine was not originally formed for walking upright but for living in trees and walking on all fours; apes and monkeys do not need chiropractors. Also, consider the case of the vegetarian panda bear that eats bamboo leaves. In order to strip the leaves off the bamboo, it needs a thumb-like appendage. And it indeed appears to have five fingers plus a thumb. But what appears to be a thumb is in fact a bone that, as we can see from other pandas, has moved up from the wrist area to play its current role. These and countless other examples show that many features of the present world are jury-rigged. That is, they were not originally formed to serve their present function. Parts that originally played one function have been modified, sometimes with only partial success, to play a new function. The creationist's view that the present species were created *ex nihilo,* rather than out of earlier species, just does not fit the facts.

Why Would God Take So Long?

Of course, those so-called "theistic evolutionists" I mentioned earlier do not dispute all the evidence pointing to the truth of evolution. They think that they can reconcile evolution and theism. Evolution, they say, is simply the way God chose to create the world. However, although this view is not as fully disprovable as creationism, it does not give us a satisfactory view. For example, if God is all-wise and all-powerful, God would have been able to create the world in its present form all at once, just as the creationist says. Why would God take fifteen or twenty billion years to do what could have been done in a week? Theists generally suppose that human beings are the only species with any real value, that the rest of the universe was created as a stage for the divine-human drama. Why would God take so long to get to the main act? Even theists who are not as anthropocentric assume that a world with human and other complex forms of life contains much more value than a world with no life, or only simple forms of life. If God is interested in promoting value, why did God take so long to bring forth the more complex forms of life, instead of creating them at the beginning? The facts suggest that the force that created our world was not all-wise; in fact, it...is not wise at all, but an unconscious, blind force that works by random trial and error in accordance with the basic laws of the universe.

Evil and an All-Good God

The idea that the world was created by an all-good being is also contradicted by the facts. There is enormously more suffering and premature death than one would expect in a world created by an all-good, omnipotent being. In some cases, hundreds, thousands, or even millions of offspring are produced for every one that survives. Furthermore, while the expression "nature red in tooth and claw" may suggest an exaggerated view of nature's violence, it does reflect a good deal of what goes on. Many animals spend their existence finding others to eat while trying to avoid being eaten themselves. And some adaptations are particularly grotesque, as in the case of the female spider who devours her mate right after he has fertilized her eggs. Can such a world be the product of a good architect?

An Unnatural Hybrid

As I said, theistic evolutionism cannot be strictly disproved. But it is not a coherent and illuminating hypothesis either. It is in fact an unnatural hybrid; it seeks to combine theism, which made good sense as long as people believed that our world was created instantaneously, with a completely different understanding of how our world was formed. To have a coherent view, we should drop this forced combination and realize that evolution implies that there is no supernatural creator, that the world has created itself through a fully natural process.

Morality Is Its Own Reward

The creationists' fear that this will lead to nihilism and immorality is unfounded. To be sure, those immature people who needed threats and promises to be moral may temporarily resort to a hedonistic lifestyle. But they will soon find that this is unsatisfying, and that morality is its own reward. To realize that we are not the purposeful products of a conscious creator, and that there is no heavenly life in store for us after death, will be upsetting to those who had believed these myths, which made us seem so important in the scheme of things. But this loss is more than compensated for by the benefits of the evolutionary view, which teaches us to see ourselves humbly as one of millions of species, one that must learn to live in harmony with the rest of nature.

III. Not at All: A Christian Existentialist's Answer

The Scientific Framework of Meaning

The question "How are God and evolution related?" reflects a confusion. It falsely assumes that "God" and "evolution" are words belonging to the same framework of meaning, so that they could be competing answers to the same type of question. Both of the previous answers to the question reflect this confusion. The creationist assumes that talk of God as our creator is threatened by the theory of evolution and hence rejects this theory. The evolutionist believes that the integrity of the evolutionary process is threatened by God-talk and hence rejects all talk of God.

But "God" and "evolution" belong to completely different frameworks of meaning. Evolution belongs to that framework of meaning that we call "science." When we are operating within this scientific framework, we are asking what things are like and how they function and interact with each other. Most fundamentally, we are asking questions about causation. The largest causal question is, What are the causal mechanisms that explain why our world is like it is? The theory of evolution is the best answer to this question that we have come up with.

God of the Gaps

In this evolutionary theory, the idea of God has no place. Some theists in earlier days did not understand this. They basically accepted the evolutionary picture, but they tried to insert God into it here and there. They claimed, for example, that natural evolutionary processes could explain the development of the universe up to the existence of life, but they thought that life could not have come into existence apart from a special act of God. Once life was created, they agreed that all the species of plants and animals could have evolved in accordance with the natural mechanisms of the evolutionary process. But, they claimed, the human soul required another special act of God. These claims depended on the assumption that there were big gaps between non-living and living things, and between human beings and all other animals, gaps so big that a supernatural act of God would be required to span them. God was brought into the theory as a "God of the gaps." But further scientific progress showed that these alleged gaps do not exist. Theology was therefore forced to retreat from its claims. The way in which theology tied its talk about God to claims about gaps in the evolutionary process, and then retreated from these claims but continued to speak about God, brought theology into disrepute.

The Religious Framework of Meaning

What these theologians failed to grasp was that God is not one more cause among others, operating alongside gravity, electromagnetism, the weak force, and the strong force. God is not the answer to a scientific question. The idea of God belongs in another framework of meaning, the framework we call "religion," or "faith." When we confess in a creed that God is "the maker of heaven and earth," we do not mean that the theory of evolution is incomplete, that evolution's natural causes have to be supplemented by divine causation. We mean to say instead that we accept our lives as gifts, that existence is basically good, in spite of all its evils, and that we will commit ourselves to lead a life of loving responsibility.

And beyond all this, we mean to say that the whole network of natural causes is contingent. The fact that it exists at all is a great mystery, a cause for wonder. The word *God* reminds us of the wonder that anything exists at all.

Creationists and Atheists Both Err

The mistake of creationism is to fail to understand that the idea of God serves these functions, rather than an explanatory function. The creationist tries to put the idea of God into the scientific framework, where there is no room for it, and where it does not belong anyway. The mistake of the atheists is to assume that the scientific framework is the only framework of meaning that we need. Rightly seeing that God does not fit into this framework, they wrongly conclude that talk of God is meaningless altogether. What both groups need to see is that there are these two major frameworks of meaning, the scientific and the religious, and that both are valid and necessary. We cannot properly understand the world if some events or features of the world are said to be caused by God, as opposed to natural causes. As scientists, we must be atheists. But we cannot live fully human lives unless we also interpret the world and our lives religiously. In this framework, we properly see everything as rooted in God, and accept our lives as a gift of God.

IV. God as the Source of Evolution: A Process Theologian's Answer

A Naturalistic Theism

As a process theologian, I accept evolution but agree with the creationist that the atheistic version of evolution is unsatisfactory. The existentialist is right to affirm both God and evolution without affirming a God of the gaps. But we cannot do this by trying to keep science and religion in watertight compartments. We need a unified view of the world, i.e., a version of theistic evolutionism.

The atheist says that theistic evolution is an unnatural hybrid, since theism implies creationism. This would be true *if* by theism one meant belief in the supernatural, omnipotent being described by the creationist. One *would* expect such a being to create *ex nihilo,* and not to spend billions of years getting to the forms of life that are capable of higher values. And one would expect such a being to have brought forth a world with less evil in it. But this supernaturalism is not the only doctrine that can be called "theism." There can be a *naturalistic* theism, which makes more sense.

God as Soul of the World

God is not a being who essentially exists all alone, so that a world exists only because God chose to create one. Rather, God is the soul of the world who always exists in relation to a world. Our particular world, with its particular forms of order, started coming into existence many billions of years ago. It was created not *ex nihilo,* but out of finite beings in some very simple state, just as those beings were created out of still simpler ones.

The view of God as soul of the world combines the strong elements in the views of the atheist and the supernaturalist. With the supernaturalist, it agrees that the world, taken as the totality of finite beings, cannot provide a satisfactory explanation for the evolutionary process. Without some directing center, the amazing order of the world would be unintelligible. Without an all-inclusive center of experience in which novel possibilities or forms of order are contained, the novelty that has continually appeared throughout the evolutionary process would be unintelligible. The creationist is right: We cannot believe that qualities such as love, freedom, and self-consciousness existed already in electrons and protons. However, to say that such qualities have been derived from God does not require that we think of God as an external being who creates things out of nothing, and who intervenes in a world in a supernatural fashion, i.e., by interrupting the normal cause-and-effect relationships.

God's Influence in the World

We can think instead of God's influence in the world as a fully natural feature of the world, and as a feature that does not interrupt the causal power of the creatures but stimulates it. The idea of God as the soul of the world means that God is intimately present to the limited situation of the world and desires that it embody greater, still unrealized potentialities. Because God is all-inclusive, or omnipresent, every creature feels the divine appetite for novel forms that are possibilities for its own existence. In this way, God influences the creatures by whetting their own appetites. Once their appetites are whetted for a new form, it is up to them to actualize it. Once that is done, the new mode of existence must be able to survive in its environment. If it does, an evolutionary advance has occurred.

Supernaturalism Rejected

With the atheist then, this naturalistic theism rejects all supernaturalism. There are no interruptions of the natural order of things. But according to naturalistic theism, this natural order involves God-and-a-world. In accord with the Bible and contrary to atheism, there cannot be a world without God. And contrary to supernatural theism, there cannot be a God without a world. Whereas the supernatural theist says that only God exists naturally or necessarily, and the atheist says that only the world exists naturally or necessarily, process theology holds that that which exists naturally and necessarily is God-and-a-world. This does *not* mean than *our particular world* exists necessarily and hence eternally. It is fully contingent, and started coming into being at some time in the past, through God's purposive activity. But in this view, some world or other has always existed, so that God's creative activity in relation to a world is a fully natural part of who God is.

Hence, the creationist's claim that "theistic evolutionism" implies the self-contradictory idea of "supernatural naturalism" is not true. Theism does not necessarily imply supernaturalism; it implies only a rejection of *atheistic* naturalism. Theism is not incompatible with naturalism as such; there can be a theistic naturalism, or naturalistic theism.

The Value of Every Creature

Another point of concern is the relation of humanity to the rest of nature. As the atheistic naturalist says, we must reject an anthropocentric, arrogant view that we are the only creatures with intrinsic value. The rest of creation is not here for us, to be dominated and exploited. We should think of every creature as having value for itself and as being cherished by its creator.

However, this view does *not* mean we need to regard all creatures as being of *equal* value, as if a dog were of no more value than the fleas that are irritating it, or that the human being is of no more intrinsic value than a dog. We can think of a *gradation* of intrinsic value without dualistically thinking of the rest of nature as mere objects. This gradation of value provides an understanding of the meaning reflected in the evolutionary process, for we can see the divine aim as that of bringing forth creatures with more and more intrinsic value. The fact that this process has occurred so slowly, so fitfully, and with so many blind alleys and so much waste does not contradict theism of the naturalist sort, since this view says that God's power is persuasive, not coercive. That is, God cannot unilaterally control the speed, the direction, and the details of the process. God's power is the creative power to evoke, to stimulate, to propose, to guide—not the power to control or prevent.

Meaning in the World

Naturalistic theism, hence, answers the creationist's strongest objections to atheistic evolutionism, while also answering the atheist's strongest objections to theism. It portrays the world as filled with meaning and based on a divine purpose. Yet it does this in a way that is not contradicted by the scientific evidence. It thereby responds to the existentialist's desire to have a way to speak about God, freedom, and values that is not undermined by the scientific picture of the world. But it does this without trying to divide science and religion into two unrelated frameworks of meaning.

The Bible's Views

Process theology's naturalistic theism is also consistent with much of what the Bible teaches about creation. A theory of evolution was not known to the ancient Hebrews, so the Bible cannot be expected to take a position for or against it. At the same time, the creationist is mistaken to think that the Bible supports the doctrine of *creatio ex nihilo,* which was fully elaborated only in early Christian history. A few passages can be taken in that way, but the biblical imagery for creation as the divine struggle against chaos actually supports process theology's view that God creates the world through persuasion over time, not through instantaneous acts of bringing something out of nothing.

Clearly a literal interpretation of the six-day creation in Genesis cannot be accepted because it contradicts relevant scientific evidence. Fundamentalists wonder how some biblical ideas can be taken seriously, if they are not all taken literally. One answer is that it is impossible to take them *all* literally, since there are many conflicting opinions on several matters expressed in that very diverse collection of writings we call the Bible. A second answer is that many biblical ideas command assent by the inherently reasonable way in which they illuminate God's relation to the world. They may be taken as divine self-revelation simply because they are true, and because they came to us through divine influence on human minds. One does not have to accept the fundamentalist's either/or position, i.e., *either* accept the Bible as infallibly or inerrantly inspired *or* reject all its ideas as worthless. Its ideas, like those of any other book, should be accepted insofar as they prove themselves true.

Understanding God's Power

A final word: Most people, as evidenced by the atheist and the creationist, have thought of the theory of evolution as a big blow to theistic religion. They have thought of it as a doctrine that falsified biblical religion, or at least forced it to retreat to a weaker form of theism. However, the theory of evolution has in reality been the best gift the natural sciences have ever given to theistic religion. Why? Because, in a pre-evolutionary context, the theist virtually had to be what is now called a creationist; that is, to hold that the world was a divine creation implied that God brought it into being more or less instantaneously. This meant that, even if one did not think in terms of creation *ex nihilo,* God had to have an overwhelming kind of power, the kind of power that could produce an infallibly inspired book and unilaterally prevent most forms of evil. After having said that God created the world in six days, one could hardly explain away the world's evils and the Bible's errors by claiming that God's power is not controlling power! But the theory of evolution changed all this. By showing that the world was brought to its present form very gradually, over a period of billions of years, it pointed to an understanding of divine creative power that is not an overwhelming, controlling kind of power, but one that works gently, persuasively, and unobtrusively, influencing all the events in the world while never unilaterally bringing about any of them. Hence, far from pushing theists into an unstable position halfway to atheism, the evolutionary picture of the world has led us to formulate a naturalistic form of theism. Because this form of theism is not in violent contradiction with the facts of the world, it does not collapse into atheism.

Questions for Discussion

1. How is evolution related to other ways in which we see God at work in the world?

2. What are the advantages of separating religion and science, so that each has its own sphere? What are the disadvantages?

3. Should students in school learn about a variety of points of view, or should they be taught only what the teachers or the community think is true?

4. If we can understand evolution best by thinking of God as stimulating the creature's own creativity by persuasion, can we understand all of God's influence in the world in this way?

5. When Darwin's *The Origin of Species* was published, many people were repelled by the thought that they were closely related to animals. Was this a wise and good response, or not?

6. Do we expect the Bible to agree with the teaching of science? If yes, in what sense?

(Readers who are interested in thinking further about what we can expect to find in the Bible will want to go back to the previous chapter, "What Can We Believe About the Bible?")

For Further Reading

Barbour, Ian, G., *Issues in Science and Religion.* Harper & Row, 1971. Thoughtful discussion of ways of relating the two (especially chapters 4, 5, and 11–13).

Birch, Charles, and Cobb, John B., Jr., *The Liberation of Life.* Cambridge University Press, 1981. Discussion of evolution, ethics, and ecology from a process perspective.

Boardman, William W., Jr., Koontz, Robert F., and Morris, Henry M., *Science and Creation.* Creation Science Research Center, 1973. A straightforward statement of the creationist position.

Bultmann, Rudolf, "Science and Existence," *The New Testament and Mythology,* Schubert M. Ogden, ed. Fortress Press, 1984, pp. 131–144. The "Christian existentialist" view, though not focused on evolution.

Gould, Stephen Jay, *The Panda's Thumb.* Norton, 1980. Evolution viewed to show how it improvises with the materials at hand.

Haught, John F., *The Cosmic Adventure.* Paulist Press, 1984. Purpose in evolution and in religious faith seen from a process perspective.

Monod, Jacques, *Chance and Necessity.* Alfred A. Knopf, 1971. A clear statement of the atheist position by a Nobel Prize winner.

Overman, Richard H., *Evolution and the Christian Doctrine of Creation: A Whiteheadian Interpretation.* Westminster Press, 1967. A process perspective on evolution.

How Are God and Evil Related?

David R. Griffin
Joseph A. Deegan
Daniel E.H. Bryant

Two Stories About Evil

The Assassination of Benigno Aquino

Few North Americans had ever heard of Benigno Aquino before he was assassinated in August 1983 in the Philippines. Just two months earlier, Senator Aquino gave the following testimony in the U.S. House of Representatives:

> I have decided to pursue my freedom struggle through the path of nonviolence, fully cognizant that this may be the longer and the more arduous road. If I have made the wrong decision, only I, and maybe my family, will suffer....

At the time of his death, Senator Aquino was returning to the Philippines from exile on a mission of peace. He wished to offer President Marcos a deal: In exchange for Marcos' resignation and the restoration of democracy, Aquino would give him his sanction. For the sake of the country, Aquino was willing to destroy his own political future and let Marcos go down in history as one of the greatest of dictators.

But Aquino did not have a chance to make his offer. He was shot at the airport. The picture of his body lying on the tarmac is a power picture of evil: the slaughter of a decent and good man to preserve a morally bankrupt government. But instead of securing the future for Marcos, the killing of Benigno Aquino ensured the government's downfall. For it was his death that fueled the massive, largely nonviolent, public support that brought his widow, Corazon Aquino, into power and freed the nation from the Marcos dictatorship.

Senator Aquino was ultimately wrong in his statement to the U.S. Congress. His decision to pursue freedom through nonviolent means turned out to be a shorter road that anyone could imagine. By allowing the shedding of his own blood, he undoubtedly prevented much greater bloodshed. Thus, what appeared to be a great evil turned out to be a great good. Is this event not a good example of how the power of God constantly turns evil into good?

Elie Wiesel on the Holocaust

Holocaust survivor Elie Wiesel tells a story of his own experience at Auschwitz. Two men and a boy had attempted to escape from the camp. They did not get far. To discourage others from making similar attempts, the German captors hanged the trio for all to see. As the ropes were placed around their necks, a prisoner behind Wiesel cried out, "Where is God, where is God?" The chairs were removed and the bodies fell. The inmates were forced to march by the gallows. Two of the bodies had ceased their struggle, but the boy, being lighter, did not die as quickly. His body shook violently as he struggled for air. The voice behind Wiesel asked again, "Where is God now?" From somewhere deep within the author came another voice that answered, "God is there, hanging from the gallows."

Where *was* God during the Jewish Holocaust—in most people's judgment, the greatest evil of all time? How could

God—if there is a God—let such a horrendous event occur? For many, the question is even more focused: How could God permit this to happen to the chosen people? In any case, the Holocaust raises in most unavoidable terms for believers the question, "Where is God when evil occurs?" Elie Wiesel's answer in this story is ambiguous. But it can be read as an affirmation that God is here, suffering the evil within us.

The Problem of Evil

Two Perspectives on the Problem

The two stories that open this chapter make very different, even contrasting, points. In the first, a brutal murder brings about political benefits that seem to the storyteller to outweigh the loss of one good person. The events of the Holocaust, however, epitomized by the dying body of a young boy, appear to Elie Wiesel to be a spectacle devoid of redeeming consequences. Something does speak to Wiesel to say that God, the source of all good, is suffering and dying with the boy on the gallows. God is present to and in human suffering. But it is a presence without the power to remove that suffering or to resist its evil cause. This is at least one way to read Wiesel's enigmatic recollection.

The story of Aquino's murder and its consequences in the politics of the Philippines suggests the opposite view: that God is actively guiding the world's events to achieve good ends. To see God accomplishing ends in the public, political arena is to attribute power to God. That God would wield this power to cause the death of a good person is problematical, however. If God is all-powerful, God should be able to bring about good ends without using evil. Such a God seems very powerful, but amoral and lacking in compassion.

Different as the stories are, they both address an issue that has troubled human beings for thousands of years: the problem of evil. How might we describe it?

Evil and Our Idea of God

The problem of evil is a practical, existential problem, driving many people to perplexity, outrage, doubt, or complete atheism. It is also a difficult theoretical question, endlessly debated by philosophers of religion. Both the practical and the theoretical sides of the problem are rooted in a tension between the traditional way of thinking about God and the experienced fact of evil. God has generally been thought of as an all-good, all-powerful being. If God is a wholly good being who loves us, why would God not want to prevent anything that is genuinely evil, especially those kinds of evil that are simply too great for us to bear? If God is an *all-powerful* being, then why is God not able to prevent any and all forms of evil? And yet it is crystal clear to us that evil things do happen—and not just mildly evil things but horrible, unspeakable evils that we would not allow if we had the power to prevent them. Is God not really good after all? Are our lives under the control of an all-powerful but uncaring power? Why does evil have to happen, even if some good comes out of it?—the question raised by our first story. Or is God good but impotent, so that there is no hope that God will ever triumph over evil? This is a very natural response to the Holocaust story. Or perhaps there is no God at all, and we live in an impersonal, meaningless universe. Is there a way of understanding God and evil that avoids all of these unhappy consequences?

The Plan of This Chapter

Most of our ideas about God's relation to the world, and most of our ideas about divine power and love, derive directly or indirectly from the Bible. So in the first of the following sections, we seek a perspective on what the Bible has to say about the problem of evil. Then we shall consider three different contemporary answers to the question, How are God and evil related? The answers will be those of the supernaturalist, the atheist, and the pragmatist. The final section of this chapter will address each one of these answers, as well as the Bible, as it offers a process theologian's perspective on the question.

God and Evil in the Bible

The Bible and the Problem of Evil

Out of the struggle with evil and the struggle with God, biblical writers expressed themselves in a number of different traditions that developed over time. When the Bible was written, just as today, the problem of evil had two sides: the theoretical question of how evil can occur if God exists, and the practical problem of how to overcome evil. These two sides develop together, and they affect each other. In this chapter we are focusing on the theoretical question, and that means that we have to look in the Bible for what it suggests about our understanding of evil, even though the Bible for the most part is much less theoretical. But many biblical passages sketch out frameworks for understanding how God and evil are related, so our inquiry is congenial to the Bible. And our focus on the question of understanding the relation between God and evil is aimed at moving back to the practical world and freeing people to grapple courageously with the evil they confront—the same aim that so many biblical passages have.

From "a God" to the One True God

How can evil occur if God exists? We ourselves inevitably put the question this way, but to do so presupposes that the universe was created by a divine being who is both all-good and all-powerful. It is a mistake to think that the Bible always says this. In some early biblical traditions, we glimpse a tribal warrior god. Such a god, while perhaps the most powerful of the gods, was in contest with other gods and thus not all-powerful. Often the question has been raised of exactly how the power of the god of the Hebrews was related to that of other gods. Also, the Hebrews often thought that their god was calling them to do things that we cannot now affirm to have been God's will—for instance, that they should totally and ruthlessly destroy their enemies. Their god was originally neither all-powerful nor all-good.

However, it was not long before the Hebrews came to see their god as the one true God, who was righteous and who created and ruled the heavens and the earth. This simultaneous move to monotheism and to morality created a tension that is reflected throughout most of the Bible. On the one hand, the sense that God is a moral being led many Hebrew thinkers to put the source of all evil outside God. Human beings were the obvious choice, and indeed all the traditions in the Bible see the human heart as the source of much of the world's evil. One of the most powerful traditions within the Bible, the Deuteronomic tradition, regards the evils that befall us as divine punishment for our sins (for instance, Deuteronomy 28:58–68). Hence, human sin is not only evil in itself, but is the ultimate source of other evils, such as human suffering, as well. God, of course, causes those other evils, but in so doing reveals that God is not immoral, but moral, since it is good that sins are punished. However, many biblical writers affirmed that suffering was not always a punishment, but could also be the means God chose for testing a person (Job 5:17–27).

Blaming Evil on Satan

However, this view was too simple. Whereas it implied that the wicked would suffer while the righteous would prosper, too often, as some biblical writers complained, the opposite seemed to be the case (see Job 21:7, Jeremiah 12:1). Also, there were just too many evils that could not plausibly be explained as punishment for human sin. Accordingly, evil increasingly came to be attributed to a Satanic figure of cosmic scope. At first, Satan was simply one of many angels who were agents of God's will. They later were granted enough independence to formulate evil plans, although they still needed God's permission to carry them out. Still later, Satan became an outright adversary of God, roaming the world and causing evil at will. By the time of the New Testament, Satan had become the principle of evil, and many Jews and Christians regarded our world as virtually under Satan's domination.

Restoring God's Exclusive Rule

This development, while absolving God from direct responsibility for evil, seemed to many biblical authors to move toward a cosmic dualism, thereby threatening the monotheistic basis of their faith. Partly in response to the challenge of dualism represented by the figure of Satan, but also even before this figure was clearly in view, many biblical writers therefore reasserted the notion that God is the source of evil as well as good. For example, Isaiah 45:7, which reflects a time when the Hebrews were mingling with devotees of dualistic Zoroastrianism, portrays God as saying, "I form light and create darkness, I make weal and create woe, I the LORD [Yahweh], do all these things." Even earlier, Amos 3:6 had asked rhetorically, "Does disaster befall a city, unless the LORD has done it?"

This understanding of monotheism leads to the conclusion that even human sin is caused by God. Joshua 11:20 says of Israel's enemies, "For it was the LORD's doing to harden their hearts so that they...might be utterly destroyed." The view that sin arises because God hardens people's hearts is repeated many times throughout the Bible (for instance, Isaiah 6:9–10, quoted in Acts 28:26–27; Romans 9:18). Also, acts considered as evil, such as the crucifixion of Jesus, are sometimes portrayed as having been predestined by God (Acts 2:23, 4:25–28).

Don't Question God!

Another prominent biblical view is that we should not question God's works or intentions. Isaiah 45:9–10 portrays God as saying: "Woe to you who strive with your Maker, earthen vessels with the potter! Does the clay say to the one who fashions it, 'What are you making?' or 'Your work has no handles'?" Likewise, the God of Job 40:2 exclaims, "Shall a faultfinder contend with the Almighty?" This position reappears in the New Testament in Paul (Romans 9:20–21).

God Will Bring Good Out of Evil

However, the dominant answer of the Bible is surely that God will bring good out of evil, that in some way we cannot now fully understand, evil will be overcome, and the resulting good will make all the evil worthwhile. This is the message not only of numerous specific passages, but of the resurrection and the apocalyptic traditions in general. "God...will wipe every tear from their eyes" (Revelation 21:4). When we no longer see in a glass darkly, God's power and justice will be vindicated.

The Bible Itself Raises the Problem

In summary, the Bible does not so much provide us with an answer to the problem of evil as provide us with the problem. It would be hopeless to try to solve the problem by harmonizing the various biblical statements. But while the Bible does not provide a ready-made answer, it does reject a number of theoretical possibilities. First, it clearly rejects atheism. Secondly, although many biblical authors attribute to God events that we ordinarily consider evil, the development of the biblical traditions involves an emphatic rejection of the idea that God is evil. Thirdly, the Bible rejects any doctrine that would absolve God from evil by denying God's power eventually to overcome evil. And finally, although the Bible often seems to ascribe all power to God, it also presupposes that human beings are responsible for their choices and that there are sometimes relatively independent powers of evil. How all of these elements can be reconciled is the "problem of evil." We now turn to four different ways to solve it.

How Are God and Evil Related?

I. Not at All: The Supernaturalist's Answer

Evils Are Only Apparent

People often ask me how God is related to evil. Does God *cause* evil, they ask, or does God merely *permit* it?

But to ask this question presupposes that evil exists, that evil actually occurs. And that is just the presupposition that is ruled out by belief in God.

Of course, in one sense of the term, evil things obviously occur: People are killed by tornadoes, earthquakes, and disease; people rob, rape, and kill other people; millions suffer and die from malnutrition; nations ravage each other in war; and so on. When the term *evil* is used to refer to such things, then it is true to say that God *permits* evil.

They Bring About Greater Good

But why does God permit such things? Since God is all-good, God would not want anything evil to happen except for a good purpose. This provides us with our answer. Many things appear to be evil when looked at from a narrow perspective. But when we see the larger picture, we can usually see that they were necessary to bring about a greater good. This is the point made about Senator Aquino's death in the story, "The Assassination of Benigno Aquino." By itself, the event seems entirely evil until we take full account of the political benefits that were accomplished through it.

Another example: Most of us hate going to the dentist. But unless we suffer that minor and temporary discomfort then, we are going to suffer much more later on. The young child is not able to understand why the pain caused by the dentist is really good. But the parents understand the larger picture. They know that dentists are not evil, and that the momentary pain they cause is not even evil, since it is necessary for the sake of a larger good—a healthy set of teeth in the child's adult years. It is our of love and their greater wisdom that they force their children to go through something that the child at the time regards as evil.

Suffering Makes Us Better People

Of course, we undergo much more intense and long-lasting forms of suffering, as when we suffer defeat, humiliation, or the loss of a loved one. But it is just those types of things that make us better people. Knowing what it is like to suffer in these ways enables us to be sympathetic to others. War causes much suffering, but it may be that this is the way God is teaching us to live in peace.

What we normally call evil is like a dark splotch in a painting, or a discord in a symphony. Considered in themselves, they are ugly. But as part of the work of art, they are necessary to the rich beauty of the whole.

In many cases, we cannot see how a particular event could possibly be part of a greater good that could not have existed without it. This is especially true of an event such as the Holocaust, discussed in the story, "Elie Wiesel on the Holocaust." But we must remember that this life is not all. We are now like children; we see in a glass darkly; we walk by faith. Only in the next life will we understand what we now believe—that God works in all things for good.

II. Not at All: The Atheist's Answer

Evil Is More Obvious Than God

To ask how God and evil are related presupposes that there is a God. But that is just what the evil of the world disproves! My supernaturalist friend says that the existence of an all-good and all-powerful God is incompatible with the existence of evil—by which I mean genuine evil, evil that is not justifiable as part of a larger good. I agree. But instead of saying that this incompatibility proves the nonexistence of evil, I say just the opposite: It proves the nonexistence of God. The existence of God is a mere belief, while the existence of evil is all too obvious. We should not deny the known on the basis of the unknown. The only rational conclusion is that *God* does not exist. As much as I respect the view reported in the story, "Elie Wiesel on the Holocaust," my own conclusion must be that if God were real, the boy would not have been hanged from the gallows, nor would the rest of the Holocaust have taken place.

What All-Powerful Love Implies

My theistic friend uses the analogy of the all-wise parents sending their child to the dentist. I am indeed grateful that my parents forced me to suffer through that unpleasant hour twice a year. But to see how the analogy works, we must look more closely at its implications.

The parents are supposed to stand for God. But there is a crucial difference. The parents are just making the best of a bad situation—a situation in which teeth tend to decay and gums to become diseased long before our deaths. But God, according to the supernaturalists, is the all-powerful creator of all things. To say that God is all-powerful means that God can do anything that is not self-contradictory. No one can fault God for not making a round square. But there is nothing self-contradictory about teeth that do not rot. To play fair with the comparison, my supernaturalist friend would have to say that the parents had freely chosen to give their child imperfect teeth, and a sweet tooth to boot! And all this so that they could later show their "love" by subjecting their child to the dentist's drill for its own good! The analogy seems to show evil to be compatible with an omnipotent, loving creator only because the idea of an omnipotent creator was not taken seriously.

Suffering Usually Has the Last Word

Supernaturalist theists like my friend also use the tired old aesthetic analogy of discords and dark splotches. Again, I agree with the example, taken in itself. A discord near the end of a musical piece often contributes to the beauty of the whole. But that is only because we experience the resolution. The problem with life is that we usually do not experience the resolutions. People lose their loved ones and are left with empty lives. People in poverty lead a miserable life, then die a miserable death.

The supernaturalist theist says that we are to have faith that all will be resolved in a future life. But I can see no basis for this optimistic view. If God has the power to make everything right later, why is everything screwed up now? This God who is supposed to make the next world heavenly is (by hypothesis) the same God who made this world so hellish, building in earthquakes, tornadoes, volcanoes, drought, and diseases such as cancer and AIDS. And now we learn that this God also has built in the possibility of nuclear weapons that could turn the whole planet into an inferno. If such a God exists, I for one don't want to have anything to do with him. The same goes for a God who supposedly would permit the murder of Benigno Aquino to bring about democracy in the Philippines. As Dostoevski said, If I've been given a ticket for that heavenly train, I hereby turn my ticket back.

III. We Don't Know and Don't Need To: The Pragmatist's Answer

We Can't Find a Theoretical Solution

Seeing this debate between these two philosophers brings back old memories. I too used to spend part of my time trying to figure out the mysteries of existence. But I soon discovered what this debate shows: The human mind just isn't suited for finding a theoretical solution to these mysteries.

The "problem of evil" is not a theoretical problem to be solved in our armchairs. It is a practical problem to overcome. There are massive evils in the world—tyranny, militarism, nuclear weapons, murder, injustice, poverty, disease, disaster, loneliness, bitterness. The Holocaust *and* the Marcos dictatorship discussed in this chapter are only two examples of concrete evil situations we have been called to fight. The Bible calls us not to sit around wondering how these evils are compatible with the existence of God, while all the time the world's evils remain and increase, but to overcome evil insofar as we can, and to be with those who are overcome by it.

Our Faith Implies Evil's Existence

The fact that we cannot solve the problem of evil when we turn it into a theoretical problem shows that this is the wrong way to respond to it. The theologian points out that the existence of an all-good, all-powerful God is part of our faith. The atheist points out that the existence of evil is too obvious to be denied. I would add that the existence of evil is not only an experienced fact; it is also as essential as belief in God to our faith. Our basic faith is in God as our Savior. Just as God cannot save us from evil unless God is omnipotent, God cannot save us from evil if there isn't any evil!

It may be, as both of these thinkers say, that the existence of an all-powerful and all-loving God is logically incompatible with evil. But so much the worse for logic—that is, for logic when it is used for questions that it can't handle. Perhaps God made our minds unable to solve the problem of evil to show us that this was an inappropriate issue to which to apply our logic.

A Practical Problem to Overcome

In any case, it is clear from the biblical witness that we are called to treat evil as a practical problem to overcome, not a theoretical puzzle to solve. We do not need to know why God and evil can co-exist. All we need to know is that they do, and that God opposes evil, and calls us to oppose it to our dying day. One of the main things we can do is try to prevent it from embittering those it strikes. We can do this best not by giving them an explanation for why God allowed this particular evil to happen, but simply by being with them, sharing their suffering and even their perplexity. People at the edge need a presence, not a preacher.

IV. Beyond Supernaturalism, Pragmatism, and Atheism: A Process Theologian's Answer

Points of Agreement

As a process theologian, I agree with the main point of each of the three previous positions. With the pragmatist, I believe that our primary response to evil should be to overcome it, and that purely theoretical speculations about God and evil must not be allowed to divert our attention from this practical task. With the atheist, I believe that we are more certain of the existence of genuine evil than we are that any particular image of God is true, that we should reject any idea of God that is incompatible with the reality of evil, and that we should therefore reject the supernaturalist idea of God. With the supernaturalist, I believe that the supreme power of the universe is a personal, purposive being of perfect goodness, and that we can therefore live our lives in this universe with an attitude of hopeful trust.

And Disagreement

At the same time, I differ with that feature of each position that prevents it from sharing the perspective of the others. In contrast to the pragmatist, I believe that we have to find an understandable way of thinking about evil in order to sustain the practical commitment to overcoming it. Our minds are so created that their questions cannot be stilled by the advice that these questions should not be raised. A purely pragmatic faith that belittles the theoretical side of the problem of evil will lead sooner or later to a total loss of the faith that the world is the creation of a loving, good God who wants us to overcome evil. I suspect that most pragmatists would in fact welcome a satisfactory solution to the problem of evil, and that they took up the pragmatic position from the conviction that no such solution was possible.

In contrast to the atheist and supernaturalist, I do not believe that the rejection of the supernaturalistic God means the denial of God altogether. In fact, I hold that it is only by rejecting this idea of God that a truly Christian idea of God can be formed, an idea that really supports our opposition to evil in all its forms.

Evil in a World of Freedom

The key difference between process theology and supernaturalism comes out if we look again at the example of the round square. Traditional theists—that is, supernaturalists—have seldom thought that God's power was threatened by admitting that God could not do something contradictory, something that is not "do-able." God cannot make a round square for the simple reason that a "round square" is a self-contradictory idea. Even a God who has perfect power cannot be "blamed" for not doing things that cannot be done.

Process theologians carry this way of thinking further, into the issue of how far God can prevent evil in a world of freedom. If we really have freedom, then we have some power to create or determine ourselves. It is through the way in which we exercise our power of self-determination that we sometimes cause evil. Benigno Aquino's murder, which was discussed in the opening story in this chapter, was not engineered by God to achieve a good purpose. It was carried out by human beings free to choose good or evil. They chose the evil way. Afterward, however, other people used their freedom to try to find a better form of government for the Philippines, largely in response to the Marcos dictatorship's killing of Aquino. Therefore, this event should not be understood as strictly God's accomplishment either. (For one thing, the story is not over; the Filipinos may use their freedom to reverse the initial positive steps, and accumulated responses from the past may limit the present use of freedom for good.)

It would be self-contradictory (just like a "round square") to say that we are free and yet that God single-handedly determines our decisions. A "free but fully determined (by God) decision" is simply self-contradictory. But if God does not fully determine the events in the world, God cannot prevent evil from happening. Hence, the existence of God is no more contradicted by the presence of evil in the world than by the absence of round squares.

What About Natural Evil?

One of the apparently obvious objections to this argument is that it works only for human beings. That is, it explains, at most, only the existence of the kind of evil that is caused by the free choices of human beings. This kind of evil is often called *moral evil.* But this line of thinking, it may seem, does not explain the existence of *natural evil,* such as the destruction and death caused by earthquakes, droughts, and viruses.

However, that objection presupposes that human beings have freedom and other creatures do not. That kind of dualism between humans and the rest of creation was in fact largely a product of supernaturalistic theism, which claimed that God gave freedom only to human beings. This type of theism assumed that God controlled the rest of the universe directly. Process theology thinks instead that there is a degree of freedom at every level of nature. This more general power of self-determination is called *creativity*. Chimpanzees have less creativity than humans, mice less than chimpanzees, living cells still less. There is still less creativity in the individuals making up the cell, such as the molecules, atoms, and subatomic particles. But there are not any individuals, however elementary, that are totally lacking in the power of self-determination. (There are, to be sure, things that *are* completely lacking in the power of self-determination, but these things are not individuals. For example, rocks, telephones, and comets are not individuals, but aggregates. They have no dominating center from which they could respond as an individual to their environment.)

Therefore, process theology draws no absolute line between moral and natural evil. The existence of evil caused by non-human nature does not contradict God's existence and goodness—because the individuals making up the world have some ability to determine their own behavior, and thus to affect the welfare of other individuals. Because they do have this ability, the molecules in the earth or atmosphere, and the cells in the human body, can act in ways that are destructive—not to mention the evil that human beings bring upon one another.

Couldn't God Sometimes Take Freedom Away?

But at this point, another objection occurs naturally to people whose ideas of the way God is related to the world have been formed by supernaturalistic theism. Maybe God gave freedom to us, and even gave it to the tiniest subatomic particle, the objection goes, but God can take back or withdraw this power of freedom at any time. God could therefore keep the cancerous cell from spreading, or the potential killer from pulling the trigger. Because God created the world out of nothing (*ex nihilo*, as theologians say), God has absolute power over the world. It may be self-contradictory to say that our acts are free if they are totally determined by God. But there is nothing self-contradictory in saying that God could take back our freedom, or interrupt it now and then to prevent particularly horrendous evils. This would only mean that in those moments our actions would not be free.

That View Presupposes Creation Out of Nothing

From the point of view of process theology, however, this objection presupposes the supernaturalistic view of God's relation to the world, which process theology rejects. In saying that the world was created out of nothing, the traditional way of thinking says that at one time God might have existed all alone, with no world at all. According to that view, God exists necessarily, or naturally, while the world or universe, the realm of finite beings, might not exist. (See the preceding chapter.)

Some World Has Always Existed

According to that traditional way of thinking, there is an absolute difference between God and all other beings. God exists and must exist, necessarily and naturally, whether or not anything else exists. But all other beings are finite or limited, and they do not have to exist at all.

This traditional view is surely right in holding that human beings and other finite creatures do not have to exist, while God will exist whether or not we do. But it does not make sense to say that God could exist without being related to something. As process theology understands existence, to exist is to exist in relationship. The idea of a solitary individual is self-contradictory. We agree with the traditional view that *something* must exist naturally or necessarily. But we do not believe that God can exist all alone. There must always have been God-and-a-world.

That does not mean that the world that now exists is necessary or eternal. This world is purely "contingent." That is, it depends on the special circumstances that brought it into being, and it came into existence once upon a time. No particular world must exist, but *some* world, some realm of finitude, must exist. God is the only individual who exists necessarily. Humans and beetles, and the electrons and protons of which their bodies are composed, only exist because God chose to create the type of world in which such beings could exist.

Creation Out of Chaos

If some world or other has always existed, then *our* world was not created out of absolutely nothing, but out of a realm of finite beings, perhaps in a quite chaotic state. This notion in fact fits the biblical picture better than the idea of creation out of nothing. For example the best translation of the Hebrew of Genesis 1:1 is, "When God began to create the heavens and the earth, the earth was without form and void...." Process theology agrees that God began to create with a chaotic realm of events that was "without form"; the evolutionary process through which God has created our world has brought about the existence of increasingly complex forms.

When we think this way, we see that the world's creative power is, in part at least, a real and necessary part of the world itself. That is, creative power is shared and has to be shared by God and the world. The world influences God and God influences the world. But God cannot take away from the world its inherent power any more than the world can take away God's power.

Out of our belief in the world's influence on God, along with our belief in God's love, we think that events in the world can cause God to suffer. And surely Elie Wiesel is correct if he is saying that God suffered along with the human victims of the Holocaust. It is perhaps tempting for Christians to interpret Wiesel's story of God with the boy on the gallows as a case of Christ's redeeming work through suffering. But it is clear that Wiesel himself sees nothing redemptive in the episode. What happens to the boy is something that God, too, is forced to endure in its full negativity without being able to change the situation. Process theism admits that this can happen to God.

At the same time, however, process theism asserts that God never allows evil to have the final word. The suffering of Jesus, which is so central in Christian language, truly tells us something about God. God does suffer with us, and as God takes the suffering and even the evil of the world into God's own life, the way is opened to redeem the evil of the world, since the divine point of view can see possibilities that are hidden from us. After every tragedy, God begins immediately the process of healing, not through a unilateral intervention to the world, but through a persuasive call to our world to transform itself. Thus, although God never quits, so to speak, on the evils that beset us, God is dependent on our own cooperation for an effective resistance to them.

It is easy to see what a difference this way of thinking makes when we turn back to the problem of evil. Supernatural theism gave God the power to control the world completely, or at least to interrupt it now and then. People inevitably asked why the world did not seem to be controlled by a perfectly good being, and why if God could and did intervene from time to time in the affairs of the world, God did not stop some particularly horrendous events. Supernatural theism has no good way to answer these questions. Process theism, with its more "naturalist" view of the relation between God and the world, sets us free from those unanswerable questions.

God as Persuasive

But process theism does not just free us from the supernaturalistic view and its problems. It also opens a new way of thinking of God and thereby of noticing the signs of divine grace in our lives and in the world in general. The flip side of saying no to the image of God as controlling everything, or as at least able to do so, is the image of God as persuasive and evocative, of God as a lure or a "call forward" to the good.

The evolutionary development of the world over the past several billions of years, with its increasingly complex forms of order, fits the idea of a creator who has continually enticed the world to embody new forms. In our immediate experience, we are aware of being drawn to express and realize certain types of value—to create beauty, to discover truth, to be fair in our dealings with others. These experiences reflect the fact that God works continually on our experience though the persuasive power of ideals. When we become convinced that the power who now influences us in this persuasive way used this same method to create our universe, including creatures like us with the power to think this idea, we realize that this kind of power is the supreme power of the universe.

We believe that the supreme power of the universe is perfectly good. And this *theoretical* solution undergirds the *practical* commitment to overcome evil. It denies that God needlessly created evil, and also that God could single-handedly eliminate it but refuses to do so. It also says that God is always working to overcome the evil that has developed, and that God does this by persuading us, the creatures, to overcome it. Given God's effectiveness in creating the universe and us, we believe that God's persuasive power also can overcome evil. But we also know that God's success depends upon our responsiveness.

Questions for Discussion

1. Have you ever blamed God for bad things that have happened to you?
2. Has the terrible power of evil ever caused you to doubt that God exists?
3. Does it make a difference if we believe that God suffers when we suffer?
4. Do you think that we "deserve" to have things go well when we try to discipline ourselves and follow what we think is the right course?
5. How important is it to believe that God will finally and completely overthrow evil?
6. Do you believe that you have been called by God to struggle against the world's evils? How?
7. Do you always want to understand why bad things happen?
8. Why do some people strongly want to believe that God totally controls everything that happens?
9. Should insurance companies call unpredictable destructive events "acts of God"?
10. What kind of power does God have to overcome evil?

For Further Reading

Cobb, John B., Jr., and Griffin, David Ray, *Process Theology: An Introductory Exposition.* Westminster Press, 1976. Chapter 4 shows how the process answer fits within a more complete account of process theology.

Davis, Stephen, ed., *Encountering Evil: Live Options in Theodicy.*John Knox Press, 1981. Process theodicy is brought into interaction with several other positions in a lively interchange.

Hartshorne, Charles, *Omnipotence and Other Theological Mistakes.* SUNY Press, 1984. The most readable treatment of divine power by one of the founders of process theology.

Hick, John, *Evil and the God of Love.* Harper & Row, 1978. Evil results from free will, made possible by God's self-limitation, which opens the way for greater good in the long run.

Kaufman, William, *The Case for God.* Chalice Press, 1991. A defense of process theism in dialogue with atheism and traditional understandings of God.

Kushner, Harold, *When Bad Things Happen to Good People.* Schocken, 1981. A best seller by a rabbi who emphatically rejects the idea of evil as divine punishment. Close to process theology.

Lewis, C.S., *The Problem of Pain.* Macmillan, 1944. Free will, including Satan's, is possible because of divine self-limitation, which allows for greater good in the long run.

Sontag, Frederick, *God, Why Did You Do That?* Westminster Press, 1970. Holds that God's omnipotence is non-negotiable, and that the evil in the world exists because God is partly evil.

Can Capitalism Be Christian?

John B. Cobb, Jr.
William A. Beardslee
Carol F. Johnston

Two Different Experiences with Capitalism

Behold Japan!

In 1945, its cities were leveled, its industry destroyed, its people crushed and confused in spirit. In 1991, its cities are rebuilt, clean, comfortable, and orderly; its industry is second to none; its people are confident and prosperous.

Freedom and prosperity. How did the change come about? A people, determined to rebuild their land, gave freedom to entrepreneurs. Government supported them. Laborers cooperated. Capital went to work. Technology advanced. A nation succeeded.

And all this happened under popularly elected governments. Japan was ruled by law. Industry and government together cared for the poor. Freedom and prosperity worked together.

Let us rejoice in success. Why should not Christians rejoice in the success of Japan? And why should not other nations follow in its train? Democracy and capitalism go together, and together they bring both freedom and prosperity to the people who give them a real chance.

Do not Christians believe in the good life for the many? Don't we believe in freedom and prosperity? Then why object to capitalism?

Profit motive works. True, it appeals to the profit motive. But don't Christians acknowledge that we humans are a selfish lot? Isn't it a mistake to pretend that we are moved chiefly by goodwill for others and readiness to sacrifice ourselves? A prosperous people can afford to be generous in a way that the poor cannot. Certainly Christians can support capitalism!

Avoidance of military expenses. No doubt Japan progressed faster because it could rely on military defense by the United States. It did not need to funnel large parts of its resources into support for armed forces. But this alone does not explain its success.

Consider Brazil!

Wealth at the expense of poverty. Capitalism has been the principle of development in Brazil. What has it accomplished? True, it has greatly increased the Gross National Product, and some suppose this means that the people as a whole are better off. No doubt some are. Fifteen to twenty million people are now prosperous, living in the same way that the prosperous live in North America, Japan, and Europe. But the price is high. The wealth of those millions is bought at the expense of the other eighty to eighty-five million.

Ever greater democracy. Not only so, but capitalist development has driven the nation deeply into debt. Its industry and industrialized agriculture are now tied in with multinational corporations and North American banks. Brazil cannot determine its own affairs. The payment of international debts dominates its economy.

Brazil illustrates the "dependency of the periphery." Brazil as a nation is far removed from the great centers of economic power, and it is controlled by them. But within Brazil, also, the masses of people are dependent on those Brazilian economic centers that are dependent on the external ones. There is a double dependency. And to satisfy the International Monetary Fund that Brazil is financially responsible, it is the poor who must be squeezed yet again, by cutting real wages and reducing welfare programs.

Oppression and environmental ruin. Democracy in such a land, governed by capitalism, is the form by which the prosperous minority rule the impoverished majority. If the majority should find a voice and win a democratic vote, the military—as servants of economic power—would seize power again. Witness Pinochet's Chile!

And see the land! The devastation in the Amazon wrought by capitalist development. The polluted waters around the great cities. The smog. The loss of topsoil. Capitalist development spells the destruction of the environment.

Christians cannot support this!

Christians and Capitalism

Is capitalism the system through which Christian hopes for society can best be realized? One way of answering this question is by studying the achievements and consequences of capitalist development. We don't ask whether they are perfect. We ask only whether they are acceptable, whether they are better than available alternatives. Many who see the attractiveness of mature capitalist societies in Western Europe, Japan, and North America say "yes." They note the conditions of the people in the USSR and Eastern Europe and the recent movements toward a market-based economy there, and they see that they are at present both less prosperous and less free. They can argue for strong support of capitalism by people of goodwill, including Christians.

Dismay at the High Price

Others are more impressed by the high price paid for capitalist achievements. Capitalism seems to require that a large number of people live and work at the boundaries of subsistence. In earlier times, these were the workers in the great capitalist powers themselves. Today, they are more often the peoples of other lands. To these observers, the prosperity of masses of people in the great centers of capitalist power is purchased at the cost of increasing misery in much of the rest of the world.

Yet Isn't There Progress?

Supporters of capitalism see matters quite differently. In their view, the "developing" nations are on their way to sharing in the prosperity of the developed ones. Some, such as South Korea, Taiwan, Hong Kong, and Singapore, are far along toward success. Most of the others are progressing. This is proven by the Gross National Product statistics. Almost all countries are growing by this measure.

Figures Are Misleading

Critics of capitalism note that these figures show only that total production has increased. They do not take into account the loss of forests and topsoil and other natural resources, the breakdown of traditional communities, the growth of slums, the loss of human independence, or the increased dominance of the military. In their view, the masses of people are worse off than before.

What About the Future?

Probably the deepest question is that of the future. Many agree that there can be no capitalist development without present sacrifice for future growth. But supporters are convinced that in the long run this sacrifice will lead all the nations who follow this road to prosperity. Opponents believe that for much of the world, the collapse of traditional societies and ecosystems brought about by capitalist development points to a future foreshadowed now in Ethiopia—catastrophe followed by catastrophe engulfing more and more of humanity.

Other Questions About Capitalism?

Confronted by such deeply opposed expectations about the effects of continued capitalist development, Christians may be forced to ask other questions about capitalism. Is it desirable to have an economic system based on capitalist views of human nature? Would it be better to have a system that directly encouraged social concern and concern for the natural world? Or have we learned from the Marxist experiment that every effort to build a system on an idealistic view of human motivation ends up with coercion? Should we accept capitalism with all its faults on the grounds that every other system is worse?

Rich and Poor in the Bible

Exodus Is the Key

The overall story line that holds the Bible together is the story of God's deliverance of a poor and oppressed people. The book of Exodus is the key to this story. It tells us that God has seen the oppression of God's people and has heard their cry and knows their suffering, and has come down to deliver them (Exodus 3:7–8). As they struggled for survival in their land, the Hebrews kept a strong sense of their mutual interdependence and relatedness. They tried to maintain a society with relative equality of wealth and to share the responsibility for their common economic life together. They did this in the face of a Canaanite society that accepted economic inequality and the rights of an aristocratic class. But the victory of the Hebrews over the Canaanites and the establishment of a kingdom by David had the ironic result that inequality of wealth and power came to be a regular part of Hebrew life.

Concern for the Poor and Oppressed

But these inequalities were never accepted without protest. The Torah or Law shows people how to recognize their interdependence and support one another. It shows special care for those in the society who were without power (widows and orphans). A major theme of the prophets is the protest against economic oppression (the story of Naboth's vineyard, 1 Kings 21; compare also Amos 2:6–8, 5:10–13; Isaiah 5:8–10). In the New Testament the story of deliverance continues, with the same concern for the poor that marked the biblical tradition all along. Luke's beatitude, "Blessed are you who are poor" (Luke 6:20), with the woe, "Woe to you who are rich" (Luke 6:24), make the point, as well as the harsh words of Jesus, "How hard it will be for those who have wealth to enter the kingdom of God" (Mark 10:23).

Out of the long story of God's work of delivering the poor and the oppressed, we see a theme of human interdependence. Wealth is deceptive because it tends to make people forget their connection with the whole of the human community.

Prosperity as Reward

This is not all that the Bible says about rich and poor. There is another theme in the Bible that says that God rewards the good with well-being and prosperity. "If you will only obey the LORD your God,...the LORD will open for you his rich storehouse, the heavens...to bless all your undertakings.... The LORD will make you the head, and not the tail" (Deuteronomy 28:1,12,13). The book of Deuteronomy is speaking not of the individual successful person but of the prosperity of a united and cooperative people. Elsewhere, similar promises are made to the individual person: "A slack hand causes poverty, but the hand of the diligent makes rich" (Proverbs 10:4).

How Complete Is God's Redemption?

How do these themes relate to each other? One theme says that God struggles along with the oppressed to bring about their deliverance. The other says that God favors the just and hardworking with riches. A clue is the question, How far along are we in the story of God's work of redemption? If God has righted the wrongs that made God's deliverance necessary, and the world is working as it should, then the good gifts of prosperity are flowing to the good and righteous. But if the deliverance of the poor from injustice is not very far along, if redemption is incomplete, then the equation of goodness and prosperity does not work, and the purpose of God must be seen especially in the deliverance of the poor.

Easy to Think That the Exodus Is Over

There is a natural tendency of those who are well off to believe that the story of redemption is well advanced, and that the present arrangements of society are working well. In the language of Hebrew Scriptures, it is easy to think that the struggle of the Exodus is over and we are now living in the promised land. This tendency is greatly strengthened by the kind of religion that thinks of salvation as an inward change, which does not turn outward to the relationships with others that constitute so much of what we are.

In the Bible, there are repeated protests against the notion that redemption is complete in that sense. The prophets and Jesus spoke against it, as in the passages cited above. To interpret Christ's completion of the work of redemption as meaning that the world is all right the way it is has to be a disastrous perversion of biblical faith.

Tensions in God's Redeeming Work

A closer reading of the Bible shows that the two sides of redemption are always in tension with each other. One the one hand, God is always at work and has come close to men and women, especially in the story of Jesus. On the other hand, prophetic spirits have had to remind believers, again and again, that the story has not reached its end. Believers are always called by God to join in the work of remaking the world, and of entering into that remaking by finding out what it is like to identify with the poor and oppressed. The things that make life comfortable are good, and God wants people to have them. But they cannot be enjoyed in isolation. To think so is to lose sight of the meaning of the story of God's redemption.

In Defense of Free-Market Capitalism

In recent years, there has been a resurgence of support for old-fashioned "free-market" or "laissez faire" capitalism. This is the form of capitalism that affirms a minimum of government regulation and a maximum of individual freedom. What is the argument of supporters of capitalism?

Capitalism Is Realistic

At the foundation of capitalism is the clear-eyed acknowledgment that human individuals act primarily in their own self-interest. The miracle of free-market capitalism is that it has found a way to harness this self-interest to serve the whole society. It was Adam Smith who pointed out that when individuals were left free to pursue their own interests in a free market, everyone came out ahead and the whole society was better off. As Smith remarked in *The Wealth of Nations*, "It is not from the benevolence of the butcher, the brewer, or the baker, that we expect our dinner, but from their regard to their own interest" (Random House, 1937 [original: 1776], p. 14). The reason society benefits from free-market capitalism is that the capitalist system harnesses individual self-interest to produce more goods more efficiently and creatively than any system yet devised. Best of all, capitalism does this by promoting individual freedom.

Capitalism Is Efficient

No system is more efficient than capitalism, in at least three ways. First, because individuals are left free to pursue their own advantage, they have the most powerful incentive known to work hard, to take risks, and to tailor their decisions to the actual conditions of the market. Secondly, because the market is left free, it is able to respond quickly and efficiently according to the laws of supply and demand. Capitalist nations avoid the problem, common in socialist nations, of having gluts of unwanted goods and shortages of desired goods—such as piles of knickers gathering dust while everyone wants blue jeans. Thirdly, the profit motive provides a powerful incentive constantly to find improved methods of production. Consequently, the efficiency of labor—what one person can produce in an hour's work—is phenomenal in capitalism. Where 80 percent of Americans were once tied down to farming, today we need only 5 percent to produce far more food.

Capitalism Unleashes Creativity

Again, the profit motive provides the incentive, and capitalism encourages entrepreneurship, technological innovation—problem solving of all kinds. Every time the system has seemed to reach a "limit," entrepreneurs and scientists have found a way to shoot past it. Demand creates its own supply, or, incentive is the mother of invention. For example, as the source of oil during the last century, whales, became scarce, oil was discovered in the ground. Now, as petroleum becomes scarce, nuclear power is being developed. As heavy industry has been shifted out of the United States to cheaper overseas production, entrepreneurs have developed computer technology far in advance of other nations—creating thousands of new, more exciting jobs in a clean industry.

Capitalism Is Productive

The capitalist method of leaving individuals free to pursue their own interests in the market combines incentive, efficiency, and creativity to result in the most productive economic system ever devised. North American agriculture has become the bread basket of the world. In fact, it is *too* productive; our agricultural problems stem from our ability to produce too much rather than too little. A happy problem, when so many nations cannot feed themselves! Capitalism is like a train climbing a mountain. Yes, it does generate inequality, and those who take best advantages of its opportunities are far ahead. But even the worst-off members of society, though far behind, are being pulled along by the engine of growth. The standard of poverty has steadily risen in capitalist nations. Food, clothing, and shelter used to mean bread, two sets of clothes (work and Sunday best), and a shack with an outhouse. Today, in much of the United States, it means a variety of foods, colorful clothing, and an apartment with indoor plumbing (hot water!), telephone, color television set, and car! To much of the world, this is riches, and it is the reason millions of immigrants continue to flock to the United States.

Above All, Capitalism Is Freedom

Capitalist efficiency, creativity, and productivity all depend on individual freedom. When a central government intervenes too much—setting up artificial restrictions and making the decisions about prices, wages, and production—the result is inefficient use of resources, the dampening of creativity, and the loss of the incentive to work hard. Just compare the Soviet economy to the U.S. economy. Or compare China's economy in the eighties, when individuals gained more freedom, with the days of backyard steel furnaces during the "Great Leap Forward." Individuals know best how to promote their own interests, and capitalism works best when they are left free to do it. Capitalism is thus non-paternalistic—not presuming to decide for the people what their own self-interest is. Is it any accident that feminism is strongest in the United States, the most capitalist of nations? Capitalism needs individuals who are free: free to buy what they please, free to move to the best job, free to seek the best education of which they are capable, free to pursue innovative research and invention, free to take entrepreneurial risks, free to enjoy the fruits of their efforts. Capitalism is an adventure in freedom that benefits the whole world.

The Socialist Alternative

Varieties of Socialism

Much of the world is socialist, despite the move away from a centrally controlled "communism." We must take this option seriously. Of course, there are many kinds of socialism. Democratic socialism exists in Sweden, as this is being written, and did in England during the Labor Party's government some years ago. "Communism" is the name we usually use for centralized, rigorously controlled state socialism, as until recently in Russia and Eastern Europe and in China. In other parts of the world, there are socialist patterns that do not fit either of these descriptions. But we should never forget that many measures that we take for granted in the United States, such as Social Security and unemployment insurance, were originally advocated by socialists and denounced as socialist by those who opposed them.

Socialism Tries to Humanize Society

The biblical vision, as we have seen, was of a society of human beings freely giving of themselves to each other, in equality and mutual aid. In this vision, human creativity was to be turned primarily toward human relations and toward making them just. Because the poor know how far their world is from being a free and equal society, this biblical prophetic vision (together with other visions of justice) has repeatedly stimulated efforts at reform or revolution. Modern socialism grew up as an effort to humanize early industrial society. The growth of mass production in factories was uprooting people from their traditional homes, putting them to work for punishingly long hours, often under inhuman conditions, and very often exploiting those with the least power in society: women and children. A vision of workers taking responsibility for the conditions of their work and pay was at the heart of early modern socialism.

Class Conflict or Democratic Change?

Socialists divided long ago between those who believed that industrial society could be transformed within the political processes of modern democracy and those who followed Karl Marx in the belief that an unavoidable class conflict and revolution were the path to a better world. The class conflict was seen as part of an inevitable historical process in which capitalism would be replaced by socialism. But men and women were summoned to dedicate themselves to bringing about the change; that was part of the process.

Why Violent Revolution?

We who live in capitalist countries often focus on the contrast between democratic socialism as a movement of peaceful change and communism as violent change. That is an important contrast. But to think about it clearly, we must see the violence on both sides. Only when we see how those who have economic power use the violence to keep it can we see why oppressed people appeal to violent revolution. A very modest amount of oppression seemed to justify revolution to the middle-class American colonists who made the United States independent of Britain. It was, however, the French revolution, with its aim of changing the whole structure of society, that formed the model revolution for modern times. The vision of a radical break and a new, more just arrangement of society is a living hope for millions of oppressed people in many parts of the world. If democratic change does not transform the situation of the poor and oppressed, they will turn to violent revolution.

Ideology in Social Life

An extremely important part of Marxist thought is the emphasis on the place of ideology in social life. Middle-class people think of themselves as free and just in their thinking, but in fact the way the think is to a very large degree determined by their economic position. Their ideas of politics and economics, and even religion, become "ideology." That is, these ideas serve as a justification for their advantages rather than being an honest effort to account for their lives. Socialist thought can open our eyes to the role of ideology in our own lives and in our churches.

Successes of Socialism

Socialist governments have been able to lessen the inequalities between rich and poor. In countries not extensively industrialized, they often made tremendous improvements in literacy and public health. In Nicaragua, for instance, the socialist government made great strides in these fields that were largely ignored in much of the United States press.

Though modern socialism was invented to improve conditions in industrialized countries, it has been adopted mostly by countries that are not extensively industrialized. (Russia was industrialized under communism.) This shows its success under various conditions. The goal of a better life together is the socialist goal, which is being pursued vigorously in very different parts of the world.

A Theological Response: An Economy for Persons-in-Community

Does Christian theology have anything to say about these questions so important for our world? Surely it must. Yet it has, on the whole, been strangely silent. Some have thought that Christians should simply announce ideals and they should be realized. But is such a separation of ends and means acceptable to Christians?

Biblical View of Human Life

Many theologians do not think so, and process theologians are among them. The Bible gives us something more than a list of ideals. It also provides us with a way of thinking and especially a way of understanding human beings, human communities, and human history in the context of God's whole creation. We cannot find a list of rules in the Bible for the solution of complex social problems. But when we look at contemporary problems from a Christian perspective, we see needs and possibilities that do not appear so clearly from other points of view.

Capitalist and Socialist Views

Consider the way human beings are viewed in capitalism and socialism. In the former, they are seen quite individualistically. Often it is the household and the corporation rather than the individual that are in view, but even then the model by which they are understood is taken from the free, rational, individual seeking to meet individual needs and desires. It is the free competition among these individuals that constitutes the ideal market.

In the latter, individuals almost disappear. Their place is taken by classes. In the Marxist form, the need is for the proletariat, by far the largest class, to take power from the bourgeoisie. The government is to embody and implement the will of the proletariat. Although the ultimate goal is to provide complete freedom and prosperity for all, the practical outcome is a reduction of personal choice.

Paul's Ideal

Neither of these images of the human condition seems correct to Christians. We do not exist as self-enclosed individuals competing with one another. But neither do we exist as members of clear-cut classes whose interests supersede our personal concerns. The apostle Paul provides us another image. We are members of one another and of one body, performing different functions but all of equal importance to the whole.

Of course, Paul is presenting us with an ideal for the church. He does not claim that the society of his day has realized this organic community. But even so, his language suggests that neither the image of separate individuals nor that of competing classes is a desirable one in which to picture the economy that we need. Those are ideals too, not literal descriptions of what occurs, and Christians do not find them good enough.

Capitalism and Persons-in-Community

If we approach issues of economy with a vision of persons-in-community instead of separate competing individuals or competing classes, what would be the results? For one thing, we would inevitably be struck by how both capitalism and socialism have destroyed existing communities again and again. When the capitalist system works well, it substitutes machinery and energy for human labor. Farms and factories that do not become efficient in this way close down or are merged into larger units that are more cost-effective. Workers move to other sectors in the growing economy. The ideal is a highly mobile labor force always ready to move to those places where capital can be invested most profitably. Clearly, the establishment of enduring community does not fit this system.

Socialism and Persons-in-Community

The socialist system is equally destructive of community. Indeed, in Marxist countries, the governments have often been far more ruthless in destroying community for the sake of meeting economic goals. There is an ideal of class solidarity but the individuals who make up the classes are more or less expendable.

The Christian who believes that true human existence is always being-in-community cannot be pleased with either of these systems. In neither case do people have much participation in determining their own destiny. In both cases, the indifference to community is also depersonalizing.

Economies Can Support Community

But are there practical ways in which an economy can support community? The answer is yes. Such possibilities are not hard to find. Consider, for example, the agricultural economy of the Midwest prior to World War I. It was based on relatively small family farms. Often, genuine community arose naturally among neighboring farm families. The churches often encouraged and embodied this community. Even today, remnants of this economy survive, despite the impact of capitalism upon agriculture during this century. France has adopted policies to preserve the family farm and the communities based on that agricultural economy from destruction by the competition of imports. After World War II, Japan, South Korea, and Taiwan redistributed land so as to produce that kind of agricultural economy. They have been quite successful. Capitalist agri-business and socialist communes are not the only viable forms of agricultural economy.

Even in the Industrial Sector

Some who appreciate this alternative to agriculture see no alternatives to capitalism and socialism in the dominant industrial sector. But here, too, there are other models that express the vision of people-in-community better than ever. Japanese industry has succeeded brilliantly partly by providing much more security to its employees and also by giving them much greater participation in making the decisions that govern their economic lives. Recent legislation in our own country has made it easier for employees to purchase and operate the companies in which they work. Thus far, indications are that employee-owned companies are economically successful. In the Third World, many voices are calling for patterns of development that build on existing communities and capabilities instead of importing industry that local people cannot manage and increasing dependence on First World expertise and capital. As capitalist and socialist roads to development continue to show their weaknesses, the Christian can hope that methods of self-help with appropriate technology will be more widely tried.

An Expanded View of Community

Process theologians make a further point about the community in which people live. It is not limited to human beings. The whole of creation is a community. That community is most real and most important in local areas. Our lives in each part of the world are bound up with the animals, plants, air, water, soil, and minerals of that region. These, too, are God's creatures. We have dominion over them. But biblical dominion does not mean exploitation of the subjects for the private benefit of the king. Dominion is responsibility for the welfare of all.

Environmental Destruction

When we view either capitalism or socialism with this expanded vision of community, we are even more troubled. For both, the land with all its creatures exists only for human exploitation. The actual result of these economies has been annihilation of whole species of plants and animals, the pollution of air and water, the erosion of the land, and the exhaustion of mineral resources. Collectively, we have violated God's call to biblical dominion. Our refusal to live in community with our varied environments is taking a toll on our capacity to maintain a satisfactory life for ourselves.

Sustainable Economies

To find economies that have taken account of this wider ecological community, we have to go back a long way. We can find examples among the indigenous peoples of this continent before they were crowded into reservations. Traditional agricultural practices in many parts of the world were adapted to their environment in ways that were indefinitely sustainable. Today, Lester Brown is providing us with annual reports on our progress toward a sustainable economy—while noting that to a large extent, we are still moving away from it. A Christian, concerned with the whole of God's creation, must pay attention.

Capitalism Is Not the Best Economy

Then can a Christian support a capitalist economy? If this means, "Can a Christian live and work within such an economy?" the answer must certainly be affirmative. The Christian also can celebrate the real gains that capitalism has brought about for many people. Christians do not deplore comfort and prosperity.

But if the question means, "Should Christians regard capitalism as the best economy, should they support it against all others, should they look to it for the solutions of the world's problems?" then the answer is no. We cannot agree with the understanding of the world that capitalist theory embodies. We see too clearly the destructive effects of capitalist practice upon human and ecological community. We cannot endorse it unequivocally.

Modifying the Existing Economy

To refuse to support capitalism does not mean to attempt to destroy the free market or to support central planning or government ownership of the means of production. These, too, may have their role and are not necessarily to be opposed by Christians. But they do not advance the ideal of persons-in-community. To support this ideal is to begin with the economy that now exists, whether in this country or others, and seek to modify it. It is to refuse to allow the ideology of capitalism or socialism to shape one's judgments. It is to support those existing policies that would help to draw all people into participation in the economic as well as the social and political community and to increase the participation of all in determining the policies that allow people in the Third World to help themselves rather than be controlled by remote forces. It is to support those policies that respect the integrity of nonhuman creatures as well as human ones and are sensitive to the interconnection and interdependence of all.

A Test Case: Free Trade

Let us take a current economic issue as a test case, the issue of protection of U.S. industry from international competition. The capitalist ideology supports free trade. Free trade encourages efficiency by ensuring that those companies that cannot compete will change their practices or go out of business. If textiles can be produced better in Asia than in the United States, capitalist ideology favors the collapse of the textile industry in the United States. The capital now employed to produce textiles here should either be shifted to produce them elsewhere or else invested in more profitable businesses. In the long run, everyone will be better served.

Do Christian believers in persons-in-community have a judgment on this matter? The issues are complex, and confronting them with a general model does not quickly solve them. Nevertheless, it does make a difference.

Tariffs Would Strengthen American Communities

The destruction of an industry in this country means large-scale dislocation of workers, that is, destruction of existing community. Although capitalist ideologists expect that the reinvestment of capital in more profitable ways will produce new jobs for those who are displaced, it is obvious that at least temporarily many are unemployed. It also appears that unemployment tends to rise. Our government is accepting a much higher level of unemployment now than it once did. That means an increase in the number of people who do not participate in our community. If high tariffs can prevent this, they will serve the interests of the community. They will not abolish competition, but they will focus the competition among companies within our national boundaries.

But Weaken Asian Communities

On the other hand, high tariffs (or reduced quotas) will cause real suffering in Asian countries that have geared their economies to exporting textiles to us. Our efforts to preserve our own communities will weaken theirs. We seem to be caught in a dilemma. One could argue that in such a situation we should be guided by the capitalist point that more goods will be available at cheaper prices when the market is fully free.

Alternatives for Consideration

But there may be alternatives. Perhaps the Asian countries geared to export to us can orient their economies more fully to meeting the needs of their own people. Their orientation to international trade is itself disruptive of community within them. A gradual move away from international trade to regional self-sufficiency may well benefit the people of those countries. A similar move in our country also may benefit our people.

Again, these are complex questions. Christians cannot pronounce on them without the advice of those who have studied them most closely. But we must distinguish between information and ideology. A community of experts committed to one ideology should not intimidate us as we approach these issues with differing points of view.

Questions for Discussion

1. What different conditions cause capitalism to create prosperity for the many in some nations but terrible social inequities in others?

2. Does unleashing the profit motive and private self-interest produce injustice in society?

3. Where do we see the biblical exodus still at work in today's world?

4. How has the emergence of the First, Second, and Third Worlds in the last several decades either promoted or retarded God's redemption of all people?

5. Can you think of ways to reap the creative gains of capitalism without pitting individuals against each other or against machines that are more efficient?

6. Is it possible to humanize society, as socialism wants to do, without seriously reducing personal freedom?

7. What is your own judgment of the violence that is sometimes used by the oppressed to redress their situations?

8. What are some of the signs and effects of too much individualism in society?

9. What practical action can Christians take to help modify the present economy so that it better nurtures persons-in-community?

10. Think of other economic issues, besides free trade, that might be analyzed and evaluated according to the ideal of persons-in-community.

For Further Reading

Friedman, Milton, *Capitalism and Freedom.* University of Chicago Press, 1981. A powerful statement of the case for free enterprise, showing how it can deal with a wide range of problems.

Heilbroner, Robert, *The Nature and Logic of Capitalism.* Norton, 1986. A more critical, but still affirmative, recent discussion,

Pemberton, Prentiss, and Finn, Daniel Rush, *Toward a Christian Economic Ethic.* Harper & Row, 1985. A Christian critique of dominant theory and practice together with suggestions for Christian action.

Preston, Ronald, *Church and Society in the Late Twentieth Century.* SCM Press, 1983. A reaffirmation of the Christian socialist position, relating it to current political and economic concerns.

Should Christians Break the Law?

Joseph A. Deegan
John B. Cobb, Jr.
William A. Beardslee
Nelson Stringer

Two Letters to a Church

The First Letter

To the members of my church family,

Since I will soon be traveling across the desert to serve a few days in jail in western Nevada, I feel the need to let you know what has happened, and to ask for your prayerful support. As far as I can tell now, I will be sentenced to six days, most likely in the Tonopah jail.

This has come about because I stepped across the trespass line at the nuclear test site in Nevada early this year. In doing this civil disobedience I was saying, "We can't do this testing and building of nuclear arms any more.... A decent defense is one thing, but God has given none of us the right to defend ourselves by setting up the potential for committing mass atrocities, or by threatening the very earth and sky that nurture us...."

You might wonder, why break the law? Why not just make your statement some other way? The decision for me was very personal. Civil disobedience is a way of expressing urgency when other channels seem not to be responsive to the need for change.... The theory of civil disobedience is that one chooses to break a specific law for the sake of a higher law. And then, out of respect for a system of laws, one takes reasonable consequences....

We have differing opinions in our congregation, and deep feelings. None of us wants to destroy anyone, and we all want good and long lives for our children. Going to jail is a small price for me to pay to be able to express my deep concerns. Please remember me in your prayers.

Sent with love and thanks,
May Wilson

The Second Letter

Dear Rev. Smith,

Please remove our family from the membership of your church, and cancel our pledge. It pains me to make this request, but it seems we must, given your support of breaking the law, and the general positions taken by the church that weaken our national defense and give comfort to communism.

We try to rear our children to respect the law, then they come to church or read the church newspaper and see a well-known member of the congregation flaunting it. I know she thinks she's doing it for a worthy cause, but she's wrong. Her kind of thinking leads to weakening our defenses, just when we should be strong. Furthermore, what if we all started breaking the law whenever we came to something we didn't like? It would be anarchy.

To stay in this church would be disloyal to our two children; it would be to say we weren't proud of their being in the military service. If you can't believe in America, what can you believe in? God doesn't want us to be lawbreakers. In fact, if you haven't read Romans 13 lately, we would advise you to do so, soon.

What is the Methodist Church thinking of?

Sincerely,
Mary Richardson

Can Civil Disobedience Be Justified?

Although the names on the foregoing letters are fictitious, the letters themselves were actually sent to their church by two members of a real Christian congregation. This should hardly surprise us, for today churches are often the scenes of conflict among their members over resistance to government, even resistance that may result in breaking the law.

What Civil Disobedience Is

May Wilson calls her action at the nuclear test site "civil disobedience." In doing so, she clearly distinguishes it from criminal lawlessness. In its pure and direct form, civil disobedience has several characteristics that distinguish it from other kinds of lawbreaking. It is dictated by conscience, it seeks the good of society rather than personal gain, it is done publicly, it violates only laws that are unjust, it accepts the punishment from civil authority that is consequent upon it, and it is nonviolent.

In a somewhat lesser sense, actions may be called civil disobedience even when they do not meet all of these qualifications. The law against trespassing at the nuclear test site is not in itself unjust. Yet that does not make May Wilson's violation of it merely "criminal." Sometimes civil disobedience also may need to be clandestine rather than public, to protect people's lives and freedom, for instance. Then it will seek to avoid punishment too. Perhaps the most difficult question is that of violence. Some people argue that violence can never be justified by its goals. But others say that such acts as assassination of cruel despots are morally justified; that is, these acts also are civil disobedience in perhaps the loosest sense.

God and the Laws of Nations

It does seem essential, however, that civil disobedience renounce selfishness and agree with the dictates of conscience. Many theories of civil disobedience agree with May Wilson that conscience points to a "higher law" that justifies breaking some specific civil laws. Usually called "natural law," this is thought to issue directly from God and to be our standard for checking the justice of human laws.

At the same time, Christian political theories have often claimed that legitimate government, too, derives its authority from God. In Romans 13, the passage cited in the letter by Mary Richardson, the apostle Paul exhorts us to obey governing authorities because they have been "instituted by God." The idea is not that God directly established governments in power, but that forms of government chosen by nations are sanctioned by divine approval as having legitimate authority. Some thinkers have taken this to mean that in establishing and living by their government, people automatically give up the right to break its laws, even if these may seem unjust.

A Dilemma for the Church

In light of these contrasting views, what position is the church to take? Are there cases in which the church should support those who commit acts of civil disobedience? Should the church itself ever break the law? Or must the church stand steadfastly in support of civil authority? Answers to these questions depend in the first place on whether civil disobedience is ever the right thing to do.

The Case Against Civil Disobedience

The Nature of Democratic Disobedience

The purpose of law and government is to promote the common good. The formula sounds easy, but fulfillment of its ideal is usually very complex. What is the common good? Does any one person, or one group, know the answer to this question? And isn't it true that promoting the good according to one group in society often harms other groups?

In contrast to dictatorships, Western democracies represent a form of government designed to prevent tyrannical rules of law based on domination by narrow social groups. This does not mean that democratic government is perfect, or that it never acts in ways that are unjust to some people. The best governments, like the most decent people, sometimes make mistakes. Part of the rationale of democracy, however, is that, of all forms of government, it is the most responsive to its citizens and thereby the most capable of self-correction when it does err.

Some people argue that when *any* government behaves in seriously immoral ways, conscientious opposition to it is demanded, even if that means breaking the law. Civil disobedience against totalitarian regimes is easily justified as being the only recourse citizens have to resist their governments' injustices. But is this equally true for a democracy such as our own American political system?

Democratic Institutions Are Sufficient

Through freedom of speech, our own democratic government may be severely criticized and called to reform itself. Further, it may be pressured to do so through appeal to its many elected representatives. And the justice of its policies may be checked in our courts against the U.S. Constitution, which stands as an undeniable high standard of fairness and good political conduct. Thus, since there are sufficient institutional channels to correct injustice in our democratic system, civil disobedience, even in its purest form, cannot be defended as a morally acceptable tactic to reform it.

But Is Democracy Too Slow?

Several points are frequently cited against this argument. First, it is claimed that the wheels of political justice turn so slowly in our system that great harm can continue to come to many persons even as the process of exchanging damaging policies is under way. In such cases, "normal" political procedures are not strong or fast enough. More drastic measures are called for.

But it is well worth asking whether breaking the law is any more effective against the evils it is intended to combat than established political and legal means. Often it only brands reformers as lawless and antisocial. During the Vietnam era, for example, the antiwar movement was given a black eye by such acts as breaking into draft board offices and destroying records. Evil must be opposed by good, not by further evil.

There is another significant consideration here. Can we expect governments, as complex as they are, to reform their behavior on a dime, as it were, just as soon as someone finds reason to criticize them? It is not even common for the individual persons to be so morally responsive. How then do we justify violation of our nation's laws on the basis of its slow response? How fast is fast enough? And which solution will work? Change takes a reasonable amount of time, especially for enormously bureaucratic governmental and legal systems.

Isn't Majority Rule Dangerous?

A second, more critical point cited against the sufficiency of democratic institutions to correct injustices is the inherent danger of majority rule. Many people assume that majority approval is what makes social policies "right," but this belief is hardly warranted. It is possible for an overwhelming majority to be wrong on the morality of a policy. Yet even then, the majority often has its way. Many an evil in history—slavery, for instance—has been maintained because the majority of people believed it to be right. Even the interpretation of the Constitution is subject to the pressure of misguided majorities. All this shows clearly that even majority rule must sometimes be opposed. But since majorities control normal political processes in democracy, civil disobedience is the only means in such cases by which to stand up for justice.

Conscience Is No Better

The problem with this position is that it exposes the rule of law to violation by any person who sincerely believes the majority to be in error. Democracy demands that, once a political consensus has been reached, even the opposition must comply with it. Otherwise, there can be no rule of law at all. Acts of civil disobedience are chosen on the basis of private conscience. If people are allowed by conscience to comply or not comply with whichever laws they choose, then we open ourselves to anarchy. Some people may want to forcibly stop a train carrying nuclear weapons. But some others may want to blow up an abortion clinic, exact vigilante justice, withhold their taxes because tax laws are unfair, and so on. We do not view all of these as civil disobedience, but such actions are quite commonly defended on the basis of conscience. Conscience proves to be no more reliable a guide to justice than majority rule.

If we want the protection of law against sincere lawbreakers with convictions opposed to our own, we must give up the right to pick and choose the law we ourselves obey. For ultimately, the law is one, and as a unity, it is only as strong as the willingness of the governed to abide by it.

Consider the Sanctuary Movement: A Defense of Civil Disobedience

There is no better illustration today of the moral legitimacy of civil disobedience than the sanctuary movement that has developed among American churches in the last few years. The movement, which arose in response to the desperate needs of Salvadoran and Guatemalan refugees in the United States, reached a crisis point with the criminal conviction in Arizona of several of its leaders in the mid-1980s.

Isn't Sanctuary Actually Legal?

Participants in the sanctuary movement often claim that, according to standards of the United Nations Protocol for Treatment of Refugees and the U.S. Refugee Act of 1980, Salvadorans and Guatemalans who have fled to this country are in fact here legally. These two documents both stipulate that the United States must protect and refuse to deport any refugees within its borders who can show reasonable evidence that they face persecution in their own countries for political, racial, or religious reasons.

The Government Says No

But the U.S. Immigration and Naturalization Service generally refuses to see Salvadoran and Guatemalan refugees as belonging in this category. In contrast to its treatment of refugees from communist countries, such as Poland or Hungary, the INS interprets the desire of Salvadorans and Guatemalans to enter the United States as the quest for economic betterment only. Thus, it treats them upon their discovery in the United States as illegal aliens and, on these grounds, regularly deports them to their homelands.

Though they have appealed to the "higher law" reflected in the U.N. Protocol and the U.S. Refugee Act, sanctuary activists are fully aware of INS policies on Central American refugees and of the risks of criminal prosecution they face in clandestinely assisting them. So far, churches and church members all over the country have assisted many Salvadorans and Guatemalans to enter the country, to live as full lives as possible while in hiding here, and sometimes to work out with the authorities the legal dilemmas of their situations.

In many of these activities, Christians have knowingly broken the law as the INS interprets and applies it. For some time it was thought that the government might not want to prosecute for fear of the political repercussions of attacking a church movement. But with the successful prosecution of sanctuary activists in Arizona, the battle lines between Christian conscience and administration policy have been clearly drawn.

Why Christians Are Breaking the Law

Why exactly do some Christians choose to engage in activities that they know their government interprets variously as bringing people unlawfully into the country, unlawfully transporting and harboring illegal aliens, and conspiracy to break the laws of the United States? The answer, as these people themselves express it, is that they are duty-bound by their Christian consciences, informed by the Bible, to resist injustice and to love their neighbors no matter who commands them not to. We hardly need be reminded that it is precisely the need of persons that identifies them as neighbors, regardless of the color of their skin or the nation of their birth.

Those who are fleeing El Salvador and Guatemala consistently cite as reasons for it the dangers to their own and their families' lives, which they face from political and military organizations in their homelands. On the basis of their vivid and graphic testimony and much independent confirmation, there is no doubt of their desperate need of the help that Christians and others are willing to give them in the United States. But the administration's policies make the very act of love in this case illegal. The position of the government is aligned with the injustice that is responsible for the misery of those fleeing Central America. In its creation of foreign policy regarding Central America, the State Department supports governments and conditions that oppress scores of innocent people. As though in a last-ditch refusal to face this reality, the INS then denies that those fleeing its dangers have anything to fear. Instead, it implies, they are only opportunists seeking more economically abundant lifestyles.

Opposing the Idolatry of the State

Those Americans who are choosing in the sanctuary movement to oppose injustice with Christian love, even though it requires them to break civil laws, are siding with the universal law of God as it conflicts with the will of a single government. When the U.S. legal system demands an allegiance that is contrary to ultimate moral duty, it is asking for idolatry. It is pronouncing itself to be more ultimate than God's own moral law. It asks Christians then to forsake God and to worship itself, the state, instead.

The entire church should support the sanctuary movement against idolatry of the state. We must prevent repetition of the Christian shame of this century in not having stood united in conscience against the Nazi persecution of the Jews. Rather, like the abolitionist movement, which used civil disobedience to free slaves in an underground railroad a century earlier, we must support those who are taking serious risks to help today's oppressed. They are surely justified in breaking unjust laws.

Render unto Caesar: Biblical Perspectives

> Give justice to the weak and the orphan;
> maintain the right of the lowly and the destitute.
> Rescue the weak and the needy;
> deliver them from the hand of the wicked.
> Psalm 82:3–4

Why Resist the Government?

Commenting on this psalm, John Calvin remarked, "Rulers are appointed primarily to be defenders of such as are in misery and oppressed, because they are the ones who stand in need of others' help." But it is often the case, he went on, that rulers "are more inclined to be infatuated with their own greatness, lord over others, and pay greater deference to the wicked and powerful than to the poor and innocent." Whenever this happens, Calvin added, those who are obedient to God must be primarily concerned with the restoration of God's order.

Calvin rightly saw that the repeated call for justice in the Bible is not abstract, but is a call for us to stand up for justice and to struggle against injustice wherever it appears, and if need be we are called upon to stand up against our government. It is the call for justice to which we primarily respond, when we relate to government.

We cannot expect the Bible to give us concrete guidelines by which to know when the point has been reached, at which being faithful to God means standing against the government. When we read the repeated call for justice, in the prophets, in the Psalms as in the present quotation, in the Torah or "Law," and elsewhere throughout the Bible, however, we often need to be reminded that the biblical writers are not just speaking about "wicked people," but most of the time they have in mind public authorities—what we today call governments.

To see this, we need only remember that the Bible is full of heroic tales of resistance to unjust governments. "They were stoned to death, they were sawn in two, they were killed by the sword," we read in Hebrews 11:37. It is important to keep in mind that these stories glorify the loyalty of these old believers, not their sufferings as such.

Exodus as a Model

Behind all the stories of resistance in the Bible lies the great story of the Exodus. To prepare for this, God says, "I have observed the misery of my people who are in Egypt; I have heard their cry on account of their taskmaster. Indeed, I know their sufferings, and I have come down to deliver them from the Egyptians..." (Exodus 3:7–8). This was the story that gave a foundation to the justice of God as the prophets and psalmists proclaimed it, and this basis, though seen in a new light in the New Testament, still remains as the early Christians call themselves "the Israel of God" (Galatians 6:16), and claim that they are the inheritors of the promises (Romans 4).

Does this exodus model still hold for those of us who are not physically oppressed, and who live in democratic societies? First of all, the exodus model makes us realize that much of the Bible, most of it in fact, was not written for privileged people such as ourselves. We must listen in it for the word to those who are excluded from the benefits that we enjoy.

Beyond this, we must listen for the word that frees *us* from bondage to our privileges, and sets us free to recognize our interrelationship with those whose lot is very different from our own.

Insiders and Outsiders

In Leviticus 19:34 we read: "The alien who resides with you shall be to you as the citizen among you; you shall love the alien as yourself, for you were aliens in the land of Egypt; I am the LORD your God."

In the Bible there is nothing like our separation of church and state, but the Bible is full of the distinction between those who belong and those who don't belong. Often the biblical writers simply accepted the separation between insiders and outsiders without thinking about it. But the memory of their own experience as outsiders, as strangers in Egypt, plus the powerful faith that God is the God of all people, kept disturbing any simple belief that "we" do not have to worry about "them." "They" are indeed different, whatever group of outsiders we are thinking about, but we are to love them as ourselves, even while they are different from us. From strangers who don't belong, they are to become strangers who do belong.

The strangers of whom Leviticus speaks came into the Hebrew community for many reasons. Many of them were refugees. As we consider the privileged place that a nation such as the United States has in the world of today, the biblical words about the stranger carry a sharp edge. It is up to us to bring the impact of those words into our own world.

Obey God, Not Human Beings

When Peter and the other apostles were told not to speak about their faith, they replied, "We must obey God rather than any human authority" (Acts 5:29). We may console ourselves that we are free to speak of our faith and we do well to rejoice in this freedom. But obedience to God overrides obedience to human beings on all issues, not only in regard to freedom of religious expression. We often think that the separation between church and state simplifies our loyalty, since it seems to put each kind of loyalty in a distinct place. That is not what the separation of church and state is about! It is a way of allowing for variety of belief and religious practice.

The Bible, both the Old Testament and the New, affirms that God is at work in all of life. The state is not a separate, secular realm.

It's Not All Resistance!

So far we have highlighted the way in which the Bible reminds us that we may have to stand up against the state. Of course, this is not the whole story. To concentrate on the New Testament, different parts of it score different points about the government. Romans 13:1–7 is a strong appeal to obey the government and to pay taxes; the same theme appears in 1 Peter 2:13–15. In much of Christian history, these two passages have been given more attention than any others in trying to define the church's relation to the state. We depend on the state for an orderly life, and these early Christians were eager to show that they were dependable members of the community, especially since they were often regarded with suspicion. On the other hand, the book of Revelation regards the Roman government as the focus of evil power (see especially Revelation 17 and 18)—so the early Christians were by no means unified in their attitude toward the government. They judged it according to how it fitted into their picture of how God was at work in the world. We have to do the same.

Jesus and the Taxes

In the well-known story, opponents tried to trap Jesus by forcing him to choose between an oppressive colonial government and those who advocated violent revolution against it. Jesus refused to accept this way of defining what was at stake. The coin that he asked for had Caesar's image on it, and Jesus brushed his questioners aside with the remark, "Give to the emperor the things that are the emperor's, and to God the things that are God's" (Mark 12:17). Like so many of Jesus' sayings, the emphasis is in the second half of the sentence. What is important is that we are attentive to God. Jesus was by no means accepting something such as our separation of church and state. He was saying that responsiveness to God is far more important than a neat parceling out of loyalties between Caesar and God.

Thus, this saying of Jesus, like the other passages we have cited, does not give us a blueprint for following him, but opens us anew to the call to respond wholeheartedly and concretely to the leading of God. Jesus' own freedom toward the government is all too clearly revealed by the manner of his death, whatever the details were that brought it about.

A Theological Assessment

Christians Agree to a Point

There is a lot of agreement among Christians on the basic relation to government. Almost all believe that Christians owe respect and general obedience to their rulers. Almost no one thinks that this obedience should be ultimate. Christians know that their final obligation is to God.

But what constitutes obedience to God? How can we know what God wants us to do? Some say that scripture alone is our guide. But in scripture we find varied statements and stories. Often we are encouraged to admire those who go against the government—Moses, for example. Elsewhere we are reminded that obedience to law and rulers is required. There is grave danger that scripture will be used selectively to favor the biases of those who use it.

The Natural Law Theory

In most of Christian history, the custom has been to appeal to natural law, understood as God's law. This law is seen as higher than the laws enacted by human rulers. It conforms to scripture, especially the Ten Commandments, but its wider reaches are discerned by reason.

Western lawyers have struggled with this theory of natural law. On the one hand, it seems to treat as absolute one ancient ethical theory, while dismissing all others. On the other hand, when natural law is denied altogether, the result is that there is no basis for criticizing "positive" law, that is, whatever laws are enacted by whoever has the power to enact them.

Process theology advocates a middle way between traditional natural law theory and simple positivism. Traditional natural law theory is bound up with Greek ways of thinking that are not truly biblical and that fit poorly with contemporary science. But to criticize this theory is not to say that distinctions of right and wrong are purely conventional or arbitrary. Nazi treatment of Jews and the slavery of blacks in this country were wrong, even if they conformed to the positive laws of their respective nations and states.

Conforming to God's View

Some philosophers say that what is right is what a benevolent and omniscient observer would favor. That seems correct to us. Most of them do not believe that there is such an observer. Process theology affirms that God is just such an observer. Indeed, God is much more than an observer. God feels every creaturely joy and every creaturely pain. What we do to one another we do also to God. What is ethically right is what contributes most to God.

We cannot deduce from this a set of laws that can be applied in every time and place regardless of circumstances. But we can try to look at what is happening from an inclusive point of view, one that includes the individual points of view of all who are affected. In that context, each of us is important, but no more important than are others. This is another way of saying that we should love God wholeheartedly and our neighbor as ourselves. Germans who loved Jews as themselves could not have been Nazis, and Americans who loved Africans as themselves could not have taken part in their enslavement or supported the institution of black slavery.

Although we cannot articulate laws that apply universally, we *can* formulate generalizations that apply quite widely. In general we cannot take the life of another who wants to live. In general we cannot subordinate one social group to another. In general we cannot allow fellow human beings to go without the necessities of life when we have an abundance. In general we cannot disobey laws democratically established simply for the sake of personal convenience or gain.

Particular Cases Are More Difficult

It is easy to agree about generalizations such as these. But when we try to apply them to the issue before us—the rightness or wrongness of civil disobedience in a particular case—disagreements reappear. Sometimes these disagreements are intense.

Clearly we may disagree as to whether the particular requirements of our governments are right. Those Christians who believe they are right will strongly oppose violating those rules; and even Christians who disagree with particular legislation often argue that the duty to cooperate with other citizens in maintaining the rule of law is the primary consideration. On the other hand, those who believe that the laws in question diametrically oppose God's purposes will call us to obey God rather than human authority.

Does process theology have any further contribution to make to the task of decision amidst confusion and disagreement? No more than any other theology can it provide a blueprint that gives clear directions as to when Christians should break the law of their countries for the sake of obedience to God. Indeed, process theology opposes any attempt to draw up such a blueprint. Every historical situation is unique. We cannot adequately understand it as belonging to a type of situation to which some unchanging principle can be applied. From the perspective of process theologies, the effort to decide on behavior by applying predetermined rules is legalism.

God's Call in Unique Situations

Does that mean that process theology supports "situation ethics"? Yes and no. It does in the sense that every decision must be made in view of the concrete situation. But no in the sense that there is a rightness in every situation that is God's aim or purpose for it. Process theology calls on us to seek to discern God's will in the situation, or better, to be responsive to God's guidance in the working of the Holy Spirit.

How can we become more responsive to God's call in the midst of the complexities of life? In this case, how can we decide whether God calls us to obey laws that we think unjust, or actively to resist?

There is no simple answer to this question. Process theology is suspicious of simple answers. It would be unwise simply to sit in silence asking God to pop the answer into our consciousness. The likelihood would be that the answer that appeared to us would arise out of conscious and unconscious prejudices instead. God calls us to use our minds to the best of our abilities.

Some Practical Guidelines

First, we need to assemble the facts as well as we can. But we need also to recognize that even that is not easy.

The so-called "facts" are already shaped by someone's interpretation, and which facts seem most relevant depends on the interests we bring to bear. We need to be suspicious of our facts.

Second, we need to examine ourselves. What are the interests that we bring to the situation? Are we trying to defend something? Do we have a psychological need to display our independence or to rebel against authority? Do we have a stake in law and order that blinds us to the suffering that law and order impose on others? To what extent are we selecting biblical teachings to support prejudices that have arisen elsewhere? When we recognize that our preferences and commitments have arisen elsewhere, how do they fare when examined from a Christian point of view? This process of self-examination is a form of prayer, for Christian self-examination must be before God.

Third, we need to share our judgments in a community of believers. We need to explain to one another how we are thinking and how we propose to act. We need to be willing to listen to one another as believers. Of course, many of the ideas that will be expressed may not themselves arise from faith, and these cannot have much authority. But we also will hear from other believers how their own efforts to understand the situation and themselves before God have guided them.

Fourth, as we clear away as much as possible of what blocks us from listening truly and openly to God, we become ready to try to listen directly to God's call. Process theology teaches that in every moment of our experience, God's call is real and effective. It is the call to us to become in that moment what we can and should become. It is not an answer to all of our questions. God's call sometimes may be to keep studying the situation; sometimes, to sleep on the question; sometimes, to talk to a friend. It rarely provides a sweeping answer to our perplexities. But as we learn to be responsive to God in the little things, we find God's guidance also more effective in the larger ones. Occasionally, it becomes clear that some Christians *are* called upon to put their lives on the line in dramatic ways.

There are some tests that help us know whether we are responding to God or to our own unconscious desires and fears. If we are responding to God, we will not be defensive; we will not be rigid; we will not be arrogant. Positively, we will feel a real concern both for those we are trying to help and for those we oppose in the process. For us, people will count for more than principles.

Different Conclusions Are Legitimate

What does process theology say about civil disobedience? Is it ever justified? Of course! Should we enter into it lightly? Of course not! That is what all Christian theology says. Process theology then goes on to point out that every situation is unique and that any rules that guide decisions must be understood only as aids in the process of thinking. Different people facing the same objective situation with the same rules may finally make opposing decisions, both responsive to God's call. That some are called to disobey a law certainly does not mean that all are called to disobey it. What all Christians *are* called to do is bring their decisions in line with God's call to them personally. Process theology can point to processes that are likely to make that possible, assured that the One who is foundationally at work is God.

Consensus and Disagreement Within the Church

Christians belong together, and help and support one another in making decisions about the difficult issues that we have been discussing. In spite of this, God's call to each one individually may mean that such a decision is a very lonely one, one that may even cut a person off from the fellowship of believers.

But that is a breakdown of community. The life of the church is a sharing of such decisions and a recognition of our interdependence even in difficult decisions. Our sharing of life in the church works in two different ways, which are not always easy to hold together.

For one thing, we do not expect all Christians to think and act alike. We support one another in our differences. We learn that conflict is part of the sharing of life. Learning how to disagree as well as to agree, and especially learning how to work through a conflict of opinions, is always a major task for the church, and a new task as new issues arise. One side of our sharing of life is our sharing of differences in the search for a common truth, while at the same time we organize that the truth is too large to fit into any one of our expressions of it.

The other side of this kind of sharing comes from the need for a Christian voice in the wider society in which we live. Through the centuries, the church has continually tried to witness to the gospel in this way. One contribution has been to give a religious and moral basis for the accepted forms of behavior in society. But the church's voice also may have to challenge the society's practices and aims, sometimes even to the point where not only individuals but churches as a whole stand against the accepted standards and the government that supports them. Most of us admire the Confessing Church in Nazi Germany for having stood against government policies. Most of us believe that churches should refuse to conform to racist policies even if the government decrees them. To determine whether the issues of nuclear destruction or sanctuary are of this kind is a challenge to the church today.

Questions for Discussion

1. Do you think that the church is a proper arena for political discussion and action?

2. What does the separation of church and state mean to you.?

3. How much protection does our U.S. Constitution provide against injustices supported by majority rule?

4. Is civil disobedience less justified toward our government than toward other kinds of government around the world?

5. Is the plea for sanctuary by those fleeing oppression in other countries a cry for justice? What do you think is a just immigration policy for the United States?

6. Is it possible to distinguish those things that we must render to Caesar from those we must render to God?

7. Do you interpret the Bible on the whole as taking the side of governments or the side of those who conscientiously resist governments?

8. Do you think that a standard exists for determining the justice of laws for all times and all places? Or does the meaning of justice depend on who has political power?

9. What situation can you imagine in which God might call you to disobey our nation's laws?

For Further Reading

American Friends Service Committee, "Guidelines for Civil Disobedience," *The Friends Journal*, May 15, 1985, pp. 9–10. Questions to ask when contemplating civil disobedience.

Brown, Robert McAfee, *Saying Yes and Saying No: On Rendering to God and Caesar.* Westminster Press, 1986. The responsibility of the Christian to and for the state.

Coffin, William Sloane, Jr., and Liebman, Morris I., *Civil Disobedience: Aid or Hindrance to Justice?* American Enterprise Institute, 1972. Both sides of the question are presented in debate.

McEoin, Gary (ed.), *Sanctuary*. Harper & Row, 1985. A thoughtful exposition and defense of the sanctuary movement. (The quotation from Calvin in "Render unto Caesar..." above is taken from Richard Shaull's contribution to *Sanctuary;* we also are indebted to that book for suggesting other aspects of that section.)

Thoreau, Henry David, "Civil Disobedience," *Walden and Civil Disobedience.* Penguin Press, 1983. The classic statement on civil disobedience.

What About Abortion?

Judith Boice Casanova
Jean Lambert
Marjorie Suchocki

Two Experiences of Abortion

Tanya's Story

Tanya always saw herself as the rebel, the one who didn't fit in, never would, and didn't want to. School was a drag, her parents were bores, and no way was she going to grow up to be like them or any of their adult friends—or anybody else she knew, for that matter. Although Tanya had been only marginally occupied with high school, she found life even emptier after graduation and soon drifted away from home to "live her own life." That life included, for a time, a live-in arrangement with a much older, already twice-divorced man. After about a year of an on-again, off-again relationship, Tanya discovered that she was pregnant.

For Tanya, this discovery became the turning point of her life. She struggled with the decision, for she knew that she was not prepared to be a mother, nor did she want a closer tie to the child's father. The crisis was a sobering shock, yet it helped her to see how much of her behavior over the years had been self-destructive. She aborted the child, left her none-too-satisfactory lover, and came home. Soon dissatisfied with temporary jobs, she enrolled in a night class and learned typing and word processing. Her new skills earned her an entry position in a large telephone company. Soon her diligence and intelligence were noticed, and she was offered a time-release program to obtain college courses that would benefit the firm. None of this came easily, for Tanya had to battle her own hostilities and suspicions as well as her own educational disadvantages. But although there were setbacks, Tanya persevered and has won the dual prizes of a better self-image and a well-paying management position.

Recently asked if she was glad she had the abortion, she replied with customary honesty and carefulness, "No one is ever glad to have an abortion, but I am very glad that I did not have the child."

Katie's Story

She had wanted this child so badly, even though she and Ben had two boys they dearly loved. She knew that Ben felt differently—he pointed to their already crowded small house, their limited income, and the financial burden involved. So she waited until she was four months pregnant before telling him, answering his suggestion of abortion with the simple statement that it was too late.

Katie worked with children who had severe disabilities. These little ones were subject to many colds and flus, and earlier in the spring a particularly severe virus had made the rounds, afflicting not only the children but also Katie. At the time, she was three weeks pregnant.

Now, at four months, she went to the clinic. A nurse commented on the slowness of the fetal heart, but gave no signs of alarm. But at her next monthly checkup, the doctor was there. She gently told Katie that there was a problem. Tests revealed the terrible story. The virus had affected all the developing organs, and the baby had only half a heart, no esophagus, and probable brain damage. If the baby survived childbirth, a series of operations would possibly provide marginal repairs, and if the baby survived these, a pacemaker could be inserted. Even so, there could be no hope of a normal life or lifespan.

Sobbing, she told Ben the news. He held her, trying to comfort her, his anger at the pregnancy now displaced by despair. How could they care for such a child, especially since it was Katie's employment that carried what medical insurance they had? "Katie," he quietly insisted, "we cannot have this child."

For a week she cried, great gulping sobs of grief. What would happen to her family if she insisted on holding on? And if the little one lived, how could she stay home and care for it?

Close friends were understanding and kind. There was a place several states away where it was still legal to abort. Ben drove her to the distant city.

There was a demonstration at the clinic that morning. "Murderer!" the crowd yelled, "child-killer!" Leaning on Ben's arm, she entered the clinic door.

Issues in the Abortion Question

Who Should Choose?

In one story, the decision was a solitary one. In the other, a very different case, the difficult decision was discussed with the spouse, and his view made a strong contribution to the outcome. Who needs to be involved in a decision for or against abortion?

Women and Men

We used to assume that such difficult decisions as these were to be decided on general grounds that were equally known to women and men, although in point of fact, men were far more influential in deciding. Do these stories point us toward a different view, that there are some areas in which women are especially close to the realities and must have a predominant voice in the decision?

A Sobering Choice

In neither of the above stories was the decision lightly taken. In neither case was abortion a wanted choice. Both situations were complex, with a balancing of better and worse outcomes. They suggest that we do well to avoid simple answers. How do we learn to hold all the issues in sight, and avoid an easy oversimplification? Do these two stories help us to see that difficult decisions may be a path to maturity?

What Are Legitimate Grounds?

These two very realistic stories do not raise all the issues surrounding abortion. Far from it. In neither of these cases has the mother been raped nor is her life in danger. But the view that there should be only very narrow grounds for permitting abortion is raised by the close of the second story, which reminds us that there are many who strongly oppose all or almost all abortions. We may find their mode of stating their case excessive, but their view is to be considered seriously.

When Does Life Become Human Life?

In one of the stories, the first thought was that it was already too late to terminate the pregnancy. But it turned out that the developing life never could be more than a fragment. The vigorous opposition to abortion, shown in extreme form at the end of the second story, rests principally on the assumption that fetal life is already fully human life. The perplexing question of the relation between fetal life and human life is all too often oversimplified; it will be addressed below.

Enforcing Moral Views by Law

In one of the stories the question does arise as to whether safe abortions are *legally* available. The public issue in this country today is often cast around this question. Of course, those who believe it should be illegal are strongly convinced that it is immoral. But some who agree that it is immoral nevertheless do not want to prohibit it by law. To what extent the moral views of one segment of society should be enforced on all is a complex, important question in the debate.

The Moral Issues

This chapter does not focus on those issues. It deals instead with the moral issues as such. The first story focuses on the question, "Should a mother bring a child into the world whose birth will disrupt her life (perhaps drastically) and often that of others as well, a child unlikely to have an optimum home for her or his own development, or should she abort?" Neither alternative is a happy one, but often there are no other possibilities. (Adoption could not possibly care for the numbers involved.) The second story raises the question, "When it is known that there is serious damage to the fetus, damage that will inevitably prevent the development of normal human life, how extensive must this damage be to justify an abortion?" How should such decisions be made? Who should be involved? Should each case be decided on its own merits, or are there fundamental principles that prejudge the question?

A Pro-Life Stance

Abortion Is Killing

Abortion is simply wrong. It is murder, it is betrayal, and it contributes to the ethical disintegration of society and the individual. To legalize something that is wrong is to commit a double wrong. To argue "pro-choice" is to argue that a woman has a right to kill and that she has the right to hire others to do this killing for her.

To "terminate a pregnancy" is to kill an unborn child, and the fact that, in most cases, the child could not live outside the womb is irrelevant. The child inside the womb is living quite well and if unmolested would come full term and be born. True, the unborn child is helpless and dependent and therefore at the mercy of those who have power to do it absolute harm. It also is true that whoever "those in power" are, the temptation is to use that power to enhance the powerful at the expense of the powerless—even to the point of extinction. Abortion is the choice of one individual to so dominate her offspring that she ends its life while it is still within her womb. By legalizing abortion, we as a society have made this murder the right of every woman who conceives.

If a woman by herself could abort her own child, the issue would still be murder. In point of fact, she cannot do so and must enlist the help of others to do this killing for her. Not only has she made herself a murderer, she has sought out others and paid them to do what she could not do herself. In this way, a new breed of hired killers has been created—men and women who kill legally and for profit.

A Betrayal of Natural Processes

The mothers-to-be and their surgical accomplices violate themselves and their species by this act of abortion. When a woman becomes pregnant, her body instinctively protects and nurtures the new life within. The rational choice to terminate that life is a betrayal of the unconscious natural processes at work. Abortion is a great violation by a woman of her own body (perhaps emotionally comparable to rape) and the woman who opts for it will pay a heavy emotional price for that betrayal. Furthermore, the woman who bears life within her is not solely an individual with an unwanted pregnancy. She is part of the whole of humanity and bears the future of the species. A decision to abort diminishes the whole of humanity. It is the option for death rather than life and as such is felt by the whole as a betrayal of the life force within us. The doctors and nurses who actually perform or assist in the abortion are, in a sense, destroying their own future. This kind of dedication to death can only be extremely damaging to the health and wholeness of those so dedicated.

There Are Other Options

A society that legalizes the murder of its yet-unborn generation has taken the laziest and yet most costly way out of a real dilemma. The dilemma is unwanted pregnancy. Could we not, as a society, muster the energy and moral commitment to educate our children, from pre-adolescence on, about the nature of their own bodies and emotions, to teach self-esteem and respect so that they learn to handle themselves and respond to each other in ways that are not damaging to themselves and society? Abstinence could again become "the fashion." And birth control must be made available to all who are not so inclined. Lastly, as a society, we must provide the support and resources so that every child who is born can be fed and sheltered, loved, and cherished until it reaches adulthood. Not to do so diminishes the whole human race. To murder our unborn so that we do not have to make this commitment is to become inhuman and monstrous.

A Pro-Choice Stance

A Fetus Is a Potential Person

A fetus is a potential, not an actual, person. And the basic right to exercise control over her own body and personhood belongs to the woman. These are the basic affirmations by which we counter the claims of the so-called pro-life stance.

The fetus is not yet a human person, but is in the process of becoming one. This process moves from a point of being a conjoined sperm and egg, and therefore a potential human being, through a complex development that eventually brings the fetus to the point of physical development that can sustain personhood. The abortion of the fetus is the cessation of a *potential* person, not an *actual* person. There is only one actual person involved in pregnancy, and that is the woman herself. What is being denied in the refusal of her choice to continue or discontinue the pregnancy is her own control of her body and her personhood.

The refusal of a woman's right to choose abortion pits the good of an actual person against the supposed good of a potential person. The present is sacrificed for the sake of a future that is not at all assured to be good. For the tragedy in many cases is that in fact the woman is guaranteed to suffer—as is the eventually born child—if the choice to abort is denied. The only ones who would seem to be spared suffering are those strangers who assume the right to decide for the woman that her body belongs to a fetus she must bear, but these same strangers take no responsibility to help care for the child that would be born.

A Child Is Not an Isolated Life

A child is the sum of all its relationships, not simply the product of a union of sperm and egg. If the mother has neglected or abused her own body, if she lacks the emotional or financial resources to care for her offspring, if she simply feels she cannot become a mother at this time, or if the fetus itself is malformed, the child that would be born is doomed to a half-life of frustration and unfulfillmant. Children come to this world needy; if we do not give, they do not get. Surely every child deserves to be loved and healthy, fed, housed, clothed, and educated, and thus to be given the opportunity to develop to the fullest of his or her potential. To insist that any fetus conceived be brought to full term without also insisting on relationships for growth and health is hypocrisy. Too often the "right to life" translates into a "right to misery."

Pro-Choice Is a Moral Option

We offer a moral option, a chance for responsible action. All concerned must look at the possibilities and their consequences, evaluating them in the context of each woman's situation. Whatever the action chosen, there will indeed be a price attached, for once it is clear that one must decide for or against abortion, we are beyond the time of "easy answers." However, if a decision to abort is taken responsibly and freely, then the suffering occasioned by the pregnancy can be minimized. No woman need be victimized by pregnancy. She has the right to exercise choice over her own body, and to develop her own personhood in ways that she deems best for all concerned.

The Privilege of Motherhood

Society pays an enormous price for unwanted children. Rather than insisting that every fetus be brought to full term, we rather should insist that motherhood is a great and privileged responsibility, requiring not just the months of gestation, but years of commitment. A woman who cannot or will not make this commitment should not be forced to bring a fetus to birth. Perhaps we should ask that no one give birth who cannot welcome this new one into her world. Then we could dedicate ourselves to caring more faithfully for the human beings of all ages who are already here among us.

"Where We've Been" with the Abortion Question

Three Channels of Tradition

We are not the first generation of women and men to face questions about abortion. Modern medicine has made abortions both effective and relatively safe for the pregnant woman. Because of this, we tend to think that the question of whether to carry a pregnancy to term is itself a modern question. It is not. It has been debated for centuries.

Knowing a bit about the tradition of human beings asking the question can deepen our sensitivity as twentieth century North American Christians who seek to build our own understanding and make our own decision.

The river of our tradition has three "major channels." It also has been fed by many smaller streams. Most deeply informing our conscious and unconscious responses to the question are the ancient Greek and Roman world, Hebraic and Jewish teaching, and Christian doctrines of the early, formative years. But the practices and attitudes of Teutonic and Scandinavian Europe, of African and Far Eastern cultures, and of Native American peoples are increasingly commending themselves in their own right as well as having had subtle influences on what is, for us, the "main river."

We cannot take all this into consideration consciously or we will be both confused and "stuck," with too much data to study before we can begin reflecting. Some of the tradition may affect us without our being fully aware of it. And it is worth remembering that unchosen pregnancy is a problem the whole family has had to face. We aren't the first, and we aren't alone.

The three major channels of our tradition are not in agreement about what can and should be done, or about what philosophical and moral questions are at stake.

The Ancient Greek and Modern World

Data on the social positions regarding abortion in the six hundred years preceding the Common Era (CE) come from two kinds of sources: ethical teaching and legislation. Greek and Roman views range from prohibition (Solon of Athens, sixth century BCE), and the Hippocratic Oath (about fourth century BCE), to defining the cases when abortion was appropriate (Plato, fourth century BCE), and mandating its practice in some cases (Aristotle, later fourth century BCE).

While the Hippocratic Oath apparently revered fetal life as fully human, since it included the commitment not to prescribe pessaries among other injurious and therefore prohibited practices, the philosophers found reasons of state—prevention of deformed citizens, limits on population density—adequate to warrant state-initiated terminations of pregnancy. Stoics held the fetus not to be a person, but proscribed abortion anyway. Orphics opposed abortion because of their belief in the pre-existence of a soul independent of the body.

In Roman law, abortion was considered an offense against the sire of the fetus; Plutarch (first century CE) reports Roman law approving divorce in cases where a woman "used poisonous drugs," which might include abortifacients. This respect for paternal right had a long history in Roman custom, inasmuch as the earliest Roman law, from 450 BCE, allowed a father to expose any female infant and any deformed infant of either sex. Michael J. Gorman, who reports on the tradition primarily to support a pro-life position, nevertheless acknowledges in *Abortion and the Early Church* (Paulist Press, 1982) that abortion was never punished as a crime in the early Roman republic and that "Roman law never viewed the fetus as a human being but rather as a part of the maternal viscera" (p. 25).

In the chaos of the later Roman Empire and post-imperial periods, the frequency of abortions appears to have increased, and there was an attempt to sanction against them in the law. Throughout, there is no concern expressed for the fetus, but for other factors, among them outrage at a woman's being able to "deprive her husband of children," and the reasons of state we have noted. Pertinent to the twentieth-century discussion is an observation by Gorman, "that the fetus is not a person was fundamental to Roman law" (p. 32).

Hebrew and Jewish Teaching

The Bible—the Hebrew Scriptures and those of the early Christian community—are our sources here, along with some references to the Mishnah.

The Bible reports abundantly about what the people of God, during many centuries of their existence, said about human life and its value, possibilities, ambiguities, and distortion. Almost nowhere, however, does it directly address the subject of abortion.

Only one text explicitly raises the question: Exodus 21:22ff. Here the context is a law about how to make amends if a fight between men accidentally injures a pregnant woman so that the fetus is aborted. The text says that punishment should be decided by the woman's husband, and shows that the writers were not thinking of the fetus as a fully human person with the values and rights of an already-born person.The law of life-for-life is not applied, but rather the procedure for loss of livestock or property.

This does not mean that the Hebrew Bible considers a fetal human equivalent to a cow or sheep, of course, as other texts, such as Jeremiah 1:5, illustrate ("Before I formed you in the womb I knew you, and before you were born I consecrated you; I appointed you a prophet to the nations"). Rather, this law in Exodus 21 merely indicates that while human fetal life had value, its value was not weighted as heavily as that of a born human.

From other passages in Hebrew Scripture, one may imagine that the significant difference those writers assumed was that of "breath." The *nephesh,* by which a human being comes to reflect God's image, to be a person, to be a relational (call-able) creature, was understood to be breathed into each born human, making her or him a person, a "living soul."

As Meredith Kline says in her article, "Lex Talionis and the Human Fetus" in the *Journal of the Evangelical Theological Society* (Vol. 20 [1977], pp. 193-202), "The most significant abortion legislation in the biblical law is that there is none." She thinks the silence indicates the unthinkability of abortion in Israel, but this view must be balanced by the observation that Hebrew teaching did not hesitate to condemn many other practices of neighboring peoples that they wished to exclude from the life of the people of God, among them idolatry, sacred prostitution, and witchcraft. The New Testament is also silent where, among the many instructions to young Christians in household codes and church discipline, abortion is not mentioned. Some believe that passages forbidding witchcraft, particularly in the New Testament, are veiled references to abortion, in that the use of herbal medicines by folk practitioners included prescriptions of abortifacients. This is possible, but it is at best a stretching of the very limited data to cover a modern attitude.

The Mishnah, Jewish writings following the closing of what is for Christians the canonical Old Testament, is quite graphic in the affirming of abortions in certain cases. M. Ohalot 7:6 (*The Mishnah,* tr. Herbert Danby, Oxford, 1933) includes this passage:

> If a woman was in hard travail, the child must be cut up while it is in the womb and brought out member by member, since the life of the mother has priority over the life of the child; but if the greater part of it [the child] was already born, it [the child] may not be touched, since the claim of one life cannot override the claim of another life.

Thus, the biblical tradition is consistent in regarding the unborn human life as valuable but not fully a human person until it has emerged from the womb and drawn breath.

However, Gorman finds that there are two schools of Jewish thought on the matter: the Palestinian, which did not regard the fetus as a person, and the Alexandrian, which provided penalties for damages to fetuses depending on the degree of their development.

The Alexandrian view was apparently based on a reading of Genesis 9:6 that has been excluded by modern translations, namely, "Whoever sheds the blood of a man within [another] man, his blood shall be shed." This was taken as a reference to a fetus. The more modern versions read the pronoun differently and repunctuate the sentence to read, as in the King James Version, "Whoso sheddeth man's blood, by man shall his blood be shed...." In this form, it is simply a text about capital punishment.

Gorman says that both views agree in disapproving of deliberate abortion, even the Palestinian. Although it did not regard the fetus as a person, he says, it was life, and as such worthy of respect and protection. While we share his assessment of the life-valuing, procreation-valuing attitude of Judaism, we are unconvinced of the particulars of his view, as he does not indicate any textual evidence for disapproval of abortion among Palestinian writers.

No doubt, methods of deliberate abortion were known to the Hebrew and Jewish people; they were known to others in the ancient world. It is probably significant that, despite Judaism's life-affirming sense of the world, no prohibition of elective abortion is preserved for us in their canonical literature. It is unlikely to have been overlooked, for this literature is explicit about other "shoulds" of life—ranging from intercourse through diet and including burial. It seems that among Hebrew and Jewish writers, the question of "elective abortion" was a disputed one, not one on which there was either consensus or absolutely clear opinion.

Formative Early Christian Doctrine and Its Development

As Christianity developed beyond its biblical roots, it brought a new perspective to the Western world. Partly, no doubt, in reaction against the bloody times in which the church itself came to birth, as well as in response to what must have been for most Gentile converts a revolutionizing sense of the value of human life, the church gave additional support to the patriarchal character of its major "forebear cultures" in the way it took positions on abortion.

To the hearts of those who spoke for Christianity, newly made tender by the vision of suffering love in Jesus, abortion came to seem abhorrent and an insult to the Father of Fathers, God "himself." The Didache (second century CE) includes "murderers of children" among those who walk in the way of death, which may refer to infanticide as well as abortion. By the thirteenth century, this text came to be translated in Latin as *abortuantes,* abortionists.

There is criticism of elective abortion throughout the formative period of Christianity, with various reasons giving for barring the practice. The familiar arguments about ensoulment, father-right, and women's immorality were developed during this long timespan.

To focus a discussion that could take pages if it were spelled out in detail, suffice it to say that despite much traditional opposition to abortion, it was not until 1869 that the Roman Catholic Church officially took its stand against all abortions, using the rationale that a fetus is a human person from the moment of conception. Civil laws also were often silent on the matter. But for at least one hundred years, civil law in the United States reflected the restrictive view of the Roman church, making abortion criminal except to save the mother's life.

The question returned to public debate in the late 1950s , and culminated in the Supreme Court decision of 1973 (Roe vs. Wade). This decision granted to the women of the United States the right to seek and obtain elective abortions through the first trimester of pregnancy (not "abortion on demand," as is often claimed). Since then, many churches have made formal statements both condemning and affirming women's right to make the decision about continuing or aborting unchosen pregnancies. A coalition of religious groups supporting women's choice in the matter, The Religious Coalition for Abortion Rights (RCAR), publishes a booklet of these statements.

What Do We Do with All This?

All this information from the traditions can inform the twentieth-century North American Christian. One important way is through observing what is omitted from the discussion. The factor not addressed in all the foregoing about these three main channels of the "river of tradition" is the matter of their attitudes toward women. We have examined all three in regard to their implicit and explicit assumptions about the fetus, but what are they saying about women?

The ancient world—now including all three channels of the tradition—varied on this point as it did on the fetus. Sometimes the woman is a seductress, enjoying illicit sex and seeking to get rid of the evidence when she becomes pregnant. Sometimes the woman is a mere vessel bearing the man's heir. Her offspring must be accounted for as legitimate and "of the right father" at all costs, and therefore a "wrong pregnancy" *must* be aborted. Sometimes the woman is a fellow human being, on a relatively equal level with the men of the society, and at least for purposes of deciding questions of abortion valued more highly than unborn human life.

Much clearer in the tradition than its (mostly tacit) views of abortion or its conceptually muddled and rather chauvinistic views of women is its teaching about the value of born human life at all. The non-Hebraic ancients, the Hebrews, and the Christians all agreed in teaching that human life was god-like, or god-imaging, or god-called. As such, it was of enormous value and not to be treated lightly. Where the traditions differed was in their degrees of inclusivity: Who were to be admitted to the ranks of the "truly human": Slaves? Gentiles? Non-Greeks? Non-Roman citizens (pagans)? Women? The mentally or physically impaired? None excluded the healthy *men* of their own society; none explicitly included fetuses.

Perhaps this will be a frustrating conclusion, perhaps a liberating one. The *help* that the tradition delivers to us as we struggle with the question about abortion is itself a *double question*:

(1) Given that human persons are of highest creaturely value on earth, whom shall we consider "human persons"?

(2) How shall we balance conflicting claims?

A Theological Response

The clearest issue in the problem of whether one would allow abortion is the depth of emotion that the question evokes. The actual decision for or against abortion involves enormous pain, regardless of which decision one makes. Further, hardly any other personal decision creates such intensity of societal response. The zeal of the "true believer" allows no merit to the opposing position; the battle lines are drawn, and those on the other side are considered not only wrong, but morally repugnant.

Why does the issue evoke such strength of passion? Can we hope to find our way through the polemics of both sides, and understand the underlying suppositions? Only at this level can a theological response deal with the problem with any illumination or hope.

Life Itself

Can it be that the issue of abortion triggers within us all the instinctive drive toward life itself? We are creatures hedged about with the fragility of finitude, and our long history has taught us well that infants are the most fragile. From many births, only a few children have survived throughout most of human history, to carry the wave of human existence just a little farther upon the elusive shore. Perhaps the passions invoked by the abortion controversy are linked to the age-long struggle not only for personal survival, but for that of human life itself.

One might imagine that those for and against abortion are equally stirred by a primordial drive toward the preservation of human life. Those who argue against abortion respond from a knowledge built throughout the generations that many births ensure survival. Those arguing for the choice to abort respond from a new sense of the urgency of survival as it is now threatened by overpopulation and depletion of resources.

The threat to life itself that is seen by both sides of this debate makes it a classic case of "single issue" moral decision and politics. A process point of view holds that it is possible to be passionately committed while at the same time recognizing the human concern of the other side of the debate and even allowing one's own vision to be enlarged and transformed by grappling with opposition. This is possible if one sees oneself as relying on the continual call to community in its variety of forms by the power in life that is greater than one's own individual existence, making possible connections that bind us together.

The Value of Life

Ironically, both positions on abortion are deeply rooted in convictions about the value of life. One side argues that human life is already actual in the fetus, and that the future or potential life of this being is as valuable as that of already-born human beings. For the other side, the life of the woman, embedded in its own network of relationships, is the basic focus to be considered, both in the actual present and in the potential for the future.

In a relational world, each existing actuality has value in and for itself, and for the rest of society as well. There is intrinsic value (immediate value for the entity or person) and instrumental value (value for other entities, persons, or purposes). As the complexity of each entity increases, its relational influence also increases in the wider social system. Gradations of value must account for the interplay between intrinsic and instrumental value in relation to complexity, and the competition between values. This, of course, is the issue in abortion. Is the greater complexity of the developed adult life sufficient to take priority over the nascent life of the fetus? Is the well-being of one opposed to the well-being of the other? The question pushes us to further issues concerning the beginning of life.

The Beginning of Life

The abortion controversy swirls around the accusation of "murder." But when does personal human life begin? The reality is that any answer about pre-birth personal life is speculative. As we have shown in the "Where We've Been" section, many biblical passages indicate that human life begins with breath, while others indicate that we belong to God from our conception. In the midst of these alternatives, what is a process view?

Human life requires the physiology of a central nervous system for the coordination of many physical responses around a centrally determined purpose. This is a biological trait that humans share with many other animals, yet it is a necessary condition for a distinctively human life. If personal existence requires a central nervous system, then the early stages of pregnancy prior to the development of such a system involve the potentiality of personal existence, but not yet the reality of personal existence. Since one cannot "murder" a potential person, but only actual persons, the language of murder for abortion is inaccurate.

Personal existence also requires rationality—we become human through our responses to one another. Who we are in the deepest sense of our personhood is developed through the formation and transformation of interpersonal relations in ever-increasing circles of influence. These relations are multi-faced, involving physiological, psychological, and sociological aspects. But these conditions require presence in the wider human society. Birth is required for the full development of human personhood.

One might argue that even in the womb, the developing fetus is in interrelationship with the mother and, through her, to the wider world of human community. For example, in wanted pregnancies the mother usually forms a bond to the developing life within her: Is this not the provision of a foundation for personal existence? Could one not regard the life within as moving along a continuum of increasing potentiality for personal existence with the relationality to the mother an essential ingredient in this journey?

A process perspective would have little difficulty in opting for the opinion that the fetus in its early, pre-central nervous system state is not yet personal existence, in which case the rudimentary relationality offered through the mother is not in itself sufficient to grant personal status to the fetus. However, once the fetus reaches the stage of development evidenced by a completed central nervous system, the case becomes more ambiguous. It may well be that the relationality achieved within the womb is fundamentally physiological; the essential elements of personhood formed through interpersonal exchange await the wonder of the threshold of birth.

Mind/Body Unity

What about the issue often raised of the woman's relation to her own body in pregnancy? Contemporary existence has underscored for us our psychosomatic (mind/body) unity. The evidence has been most striking in the case of medicine. Emotions and attitudes influence illness and are influenced by illness, thus challenging suppositions that the body does one thing and the mind another. Process thought expresses the interdependence of mind and body by considering human existence as a complex coordination of relationships. We are "embodied minds," and "minded bodies," and without this interdependence, human beings would not exist.

Given this interdependence of mind and body, the implication of the "pro-life" stance that the pregnant body must continue its work independently of the woman's consent violates the unity of the woman's being. The fetus, as intimately a part of the woman's body, is interwoven with the woman's own sense of selfhood. To oppose the woman's interests and the fetus' interests, as if they were two separate beings, is questionable. Given that unity, one must also recognize that the woman's decision-making powers continue to act as the informing principle of her being.

The mind/body interdependence adds a further complexity to the issue. Since every organism is relational, one's decisions relate not only to the personal body but to the larger body of social existence. One is also affected by that social world. The effect of this interrelationship for the issue of abortion is that there is no such thing as an isolated decision. Every decision for the self is also a decision of consequence for the wider society. In decisions concerning pregnancy, one must ask whether this birth will enrich society, and be enriched by it.

Legislation and Personal Choice

The stories that introduced this discussion assumed that a woman could have an abortion if she chose. There is a strong move in our culture to restrict or even eliminate this possibility. Our discussion has shown that the issue does not lead to a simple decision. That makes it inappropriate for legislation to deprive citizens of the possibility of choice. Process thought, with its emphasis on the relatedness of all beings, would resist any view that a decision about abortion could be a purely private decision. Others and the whole society are always involved! The decision matters to others besides the woman, and the well-being of these others also must be considered. But that is very different from saying that the decision is to be controlled by the legal structure of society. There is a fundamental pluralism in society, such that the society must respect a variety of convictions. A process perspective will lead us to press for keeping open the pluralism and corresponding regard for those whose opinions differ from our own in a matter as complex and personal as abortion.

Trust

Given the ambiguity, perhaps the best theological response is that we are called to a fundamental trust in God (or, for those who do not use this terminology, a trust in the creative power at work in us and in the world). All of our decisions ideally begin in and from that trust. This means that we make our decisions with all the integrity at our command, but that we ultimately must recognize that others, too, exercise integrity even though they make decisions that oppose our own.

It is vitally important for society to keep open the possibility of choice, and, difficult though the choice may be, it is important for religious communities to affirm the necessity and possibility of making difficult choices. Religious communities are called to compassion for those caught in the tragedies of abortion, comforting the "Katies" in their grief, offering the accepting and forgiving power of God to those who struggle under a burden of guilt, and providing a context of the community's love to the "Tanyas" who dare to choose the future made possible by abortion.

We sorely need an openness and respect for one another in public debate in the United States. We may hope that this discussion may contribute to this recognition of the humanness of those who disagree with us. The effect of this stance can be an openness to our opponent as one who also struggles with the issue in the depths of his or her being. The answers are not as clear as either side would like to say. Therefore, we are called to hear one another, and consider and reconsider our own position in the light of the other's concerns. Throughout, we must practice reliance on the life-giving power, a reliance that dares to make decisions, and also is strong enough to release those decisions to God for final judgment. We dare not damn the other, for perhaps in this ambiguous situation it is the other, not ourselves, who has the best judgment. The best Christian response in a relational world might well be humility, compassion, and the willingness to work toward social conditions that support the well-being of all.

Questions for Discussion

1. Are there legitimate grounds for abortion?
2. When does life become human?
3. What about the consequences of abortion or non-abortion, for the individuals concerned and for society?
4. Is abortion a personal or public issue?
5. Should moral views on ambiguous matters be enforced by law?
6. How does faith generate respect for the conviction of others?
7. How does knowing our history help us to decide about this matter?
8. What role do you see for the special insights of women in making the decision?

For Further Reading

Callahan, Daniel, *Abortion: Law, Choice and Morality.* Macmillan, 1970. An older book, but still thorough and probing. The author, a Roman Catholic, became convinced while writing the book that his church's position was incorrect.

Cobb, John B., Jr., *Matters of Life and Death.* Westminster/John Knox Press, 1991. Chapter 3 (pp. 69-93) is a lucid examination of the abortion issue by this noted process theologian.

Connery, John, S.J., *Abortion: The Development of the Roman Catholic Perspective.* Loyola University Press, 1977. Clarifies the history of the thinking of the Roman Catholic opposition to abortion, which the author supports.

Davaney, Sheila Greeve, ed., *Feminism and Process Thought.* Edwin Mellen Press, 1981. Papers that link the theological perspective of this chapter to specific concerns of women. See the article on abortion by Jean Lambert.

Ellingson, Mark, "The Church and Abortion: Signs of Consensus," *The Christian Century,* Vol. 107, No. 1 (January 3-10, 1990), pp. 12-15. The author studies statements by the churches on abortion, and sees the differences in opposing points of view not in the variety of theology, but in whether the human person is seen as a separate unit or (as in this chapter) as a relational being.

Gilligan, Carol, *In a Different Voice: Psychological Theory and Women's Development.* Harvard University Press, 1982. Perspective on the terms in which women tend to see issues such as abortion—care and responsibility rather than rights and rules.

Harrison, Beverly Wildung, *Making the Connections: Essays in Feminist Social Ethics.* Beacon Press, 1985. A study that approaches abortion from the point of view of the perspective and rights of women.